A Culture of Positive Change

John Iroh

A Culture of Positive Change

Author: John Iroh

Copyright © John Iroh (2025)

The right of John Iroh to be identified as author of this work has been asserted by the author in accordance with section 77 and 78 of the Copyright, Designs and Patents Act 1988.

First Published in 2025

ISBN 978-1-83538-632-3 (Paperback)

Published by:
    Maple Publishers
    Fairbourne Drive, Atterbury,
    Milton Keynes,
    MK10 9RG, UK
    www.maplepublishers.com

A CIP catalogue record for this title is available from the British Library.

All rights reserved. No part of this book may be reproduced or translated by any form or by any means, electronic or mechanical, including photocopying, recording or by any information storage and retrieval system without written permission from the author.

The views expressed in this work are solely those of the author and do not necessarily reflect the views of the publisher, and the publisher hereby disclaims any responsibility for them.

CONTENTS

Dedication v

Acknowledgment vii

Forward.. xi

Introduction... xiii

Chapter 1	Is There More to Life?............................1
Chapter 2	It All Begins with a Dream..................14
Chapter 3	You Already Possess all You Need to Succeed......30
Chapter 4	World-Changers...................................41
Chapter 5	Common Traits of Successful People...................57
Chapter 6	Has Anything Changed? 63
Chapter 7	There Is No Luxury of Time..............68
Chapter 8	You Have to Make the Hard Decisions 78
Chapter 9	Hints on Discovering Who You Are...................93
Chapter 10	And Finally..109

Appendix Success Nuggets.....................................131

John Iroh

Dedication

This book is dedicated to every person who has chosen to make a positive change in his or her living condition. To every person who, through the principles of successful living, has chosen to be among those contributing toward helping the needy in society—to those people I dedicate this book.

I dedicate this book to every youth who looks beyond the weekly binge drinking to the adult he or she would like to become.

John Iroh

Acknowledgments

I wish to acknowledge those who have come across my path in life and have left significant impact in me to continue on the path of progressive success. One of such people is a man I met while still attending the university, I was on an industrial attachment to a construction company that posted me to one of the company construction sites. I recall a discussion I had with the man who was working as a site laborer. In the short time we had to speak before he was instructed by the foreman to get back to work, the man told me a bit of his life story. He started by telling me that he blamed himself for his current situation. He said he had the option of attending a university on a scholarship, as he was a university laboratory attendant. He also had wealthy brothers who were willing to assist him should he wish to start a trading business.

He chose to start his own business and collected a huge sum of money from his brothers. He resigned his appointment at the university, started his business, bought a car and rented a well-furnished apartment. He frequented clubs every weekend and had many girlfriends. With each passing year, his business net worth diminished, he told me. He decided to get married and have children. By the time I met him he had four children—all girls. His business had collapsed and he lacked the required skills to get anything other than a manual laborer position.

I could see tears well up in his eyes as he told me that he was suffering because he wasted his youth by careless living. As he talked, I recalled a poster that stated, "If you waste your youth by careless living, your adulthood will be a tedious struggle and your old age will be regret." I had printed these words on a paper, laminated it, and hung it in my office. It has become a guiding statement for me.

I am not sure where this man is on the face of the earth today, but his story stuck with me and I decided not to waste my youth. For this I acknowledge this man whose story helped me to make a right choice.

I also acknowledge Dr. Myles Munroe, whose book, In Pursuit of Purpose, set me on the journey of self-discovery and the reason for my being. I acknowledge everyone whose book I have read and who tape or CD I have listened to that has helped me form positive opinions and make right decisions.

I acknowledge Dr. Joe Ibojie for his encouragement, advice, and support toward publishing this book. Most especially I thank him for agreeing to write the Foreword for this book.

I must not end this acknowledgment without thanking Someone special who has watched over me and shown me special love. He helped me make the right choice of career and has ensured that I have had a job since graduating from the university. In situations that others may have gone into depression, He has reached out to me and pulled me to Himself and gave me a new hope. Most importantly, He gave me a sound mind to put the contents of this book together. He is God Almighty!

John Iroh

Foreword

John Iroh has written a book that will bless many people across the world. I have known John for some years and I can say this book was borne out of his desire to help those caught in the emerging maze of life goal identity and fulfilment crisis. As technology savvy as modern people are, and as much wealth as many countries and individuals have acquired, and for all of the worldwide advances in medicine and communication, on a personal level, people still hunger for meaning and fulfilment. Daily people in all walks of life are searching for their true identity—a sense of purpose.

As part of the quest to answer the ancient questions all people eventually ask, we must look deep within ourselves to determine our destination—do we have a plan to get there, and are we equipped to achieve and appreciate our goals in life.

Many of today's cultures are focused on dependence rather than independence. If there is an easy way out, a way of least resistance—then why not take it, many ask. Many societies around the world are compromising their morals and ethical standards to win the most votes or make the most money.

John Iroh

Yes, these are trying times with wars and rumors of wars, earthquakes and fires, abuse and addiction. If there was ever a time when we needed a culture of positive change, it is now. John Iroh has set forth an interesting and insightful treatise for serious consideration. His practical, common sense look at life and how to improve it will prick your conscience and provoke you to action.

Using examples of successful people and personal experiences, each chapter is like a personal counselling session in which you can pull nuggets of wisdom that will launch you into an entirely new and exciting way of living. Yes, you can improve your lifestyle and your circumstances. Yes, there is a way to increase your financial situation. Yes, a brighter day is just over the horizon and you can take advantage of it by learning how to take charge of your life and moving forward.

> Dr Joe Ibojie
> Bishop
> The Father's House
> Aberdeen, Scotland, UK

Introduction

Some people discover and achieve success early in life while others do so much later in their lives. The road to discovery of success begins with the realization that there is a better condition of living compared to the present condition. This discovery is usually followed by a willingness to change the present condition for the better. A culture of positive change is a process and not an event. It requires some daily disciplines and sometimes a gradual shift from past bad habits.

A friend of mine who recently moved to a new job sent an email to his former colleagues, just to catch up and ask how they were progressing in their careers. Also, my friend wanted to update them about his new job.

One of my friend's former colleagues responded almost immediately to my friend's email, informing my friend that things were much the same year-in and year-out. He told my friend that there was no progress, and he was just marking time, waiting for an opportunity to retire early, otherwise retire in 29 years when he was old enough.

Many people, like my friend's former colleague, feel trapped in jobs they don't like, agonizingly waiting for retirement as it slowly crawls closer, one long year at a time. They are in daily misery, yet they continue to endure the misery rather than make a change.

While the majority of people choose to remain trapped in their endless wait for retirement so they can collect their deserved pension, others design their own retirement time and benefits package. These are the ones that own cruise ships and holiday islands. They include the owners of big corporations, the inventors, authors and industry leaders. Owners of big corporations do not depend on government pension. Royalties that these ones receive from their inventions, books, albums, and creative intellectual property could remove their dependence on pension for life. These are people who utilize the rich resource deposit in every human being—our potential. This resource is what makes the human beings different from animals.

A Culture of Positive Change explores our potential—a resource that every great man and woman has used in achieving success. The book challenges you to activate the rich, potential deposit of human ability and also provides ideas and suggestions on how to become an achiever—even a celebrity. Reading this book to the end will deposit into your life all the information required to become a truly successful person—it is the secret of every successful personality.

It is important to consider that youngsters who get hooked on drugs did not plan to get hooked. Their addiction is the result of taking one wrong step after another. This book helps people of all ages to avoid taking such wrong steps that lead to lives less successful and meaningful than what they were meant to live.

A Culture of Positive Change

Do you feel trapped in a human rat race, stuck in a job you hate? Are you living only for today and have no plan for the future? Are you living only for today with no plans to secure your future? This book helps you create the future you want. This book will make you to stand out from the crowd.

You were created to be successful!

John Iroh

1

Is There More to Life?

A certain man born to an average family grows up to be a trained medical doctor and is presently working within the national health system. He is married and has two children, ages three and five years. The young doctor is paying monthly for the house he recently bought and also contributing to his pension fund. The family manages to save enough for a vacation at least once a year. Each time the family goes on holiday, they depend on the bank overdraft services—checks are covered even if not enough funds in the account—and pay back the amount over time.

There is another man in another family who felt that traditional schooling was so much of a burden that he decided to learn a trade. Today he is a plumber and is self-employed. He is married with two daughters. He complains that his job allows him to spend too little time with his family, as he is always very busy. His wife has threatened to leave him if he continues to give more attention to his job than to his family. He manages to get a holiday once every few years when his job permits him. The man has promised his wife that he will retire from work after completely paying for their house.

A third man started working for his father when he was just twelve years of age. His father had a building construction company that employed about a dozen permanent staff. The man has continued with his father's company, and eventually the father left the management of the company to his son. The father died, and the son now manages the entire company. The company is doing very well and has some on-going projects. This man and his family live in a fully paid house. He takes the family on holiday at least once a year.

A fourth man lived on the streets when he was a youth. He was juvenile delinquent, constantly in and out of trouble. Now, as a man, he lives in government-subsidized housing. He is married and has a son. They depend on the benefits they receive from the government for their survival. Their child is not attending school even though he is of school age.

The last family I will describe is that of a man who discovered his talent for music while he was still a teenager. Today he has grown to be a world-renowned pop star. His music has made him so rich that he bought a family mansion in a prime location in the city. Although, he is only in his early forties, he has been married twice and divorced twice. He is presently dating another Hollywood star who may eventually be his third wife. He fathered three children with three different women. His first child is from his first girlfriend when he was a teenager. His last divorce settlement cost him millions of dollars. However, he is still making a lot of money from his albums and live performances.

A Culture of Positive Change

Each of the five families described has some resemblance to many of the families in the world today. Do you admire any of the families described? Do you wish that your family could be like any of those described? Maybe your answer is yes. Whatever your answer, I can tell you with confidence that there could be a better life for every one of those families. Each of the families described has capacity for a better life than they currently have. Many families live far below their capacity for better lives. There is one principle I have learned about life—at any level in life, there is always a higher and better life awaiting anyone who seeks it.

> ***At any level in life, there is always a higher and better life.***

I believe that every family in the world today can rise to a better level of life. No matter how rich a family is, there is always a next better level. Being financially independent does not guarantee a better life. Having lots of money and being able to afford anything money can buy is great, but if a wealthy person can't keep a simple relationship together, it proves that it's not all about money in achieving a better life.

Some people are on a job they hate to do just because they need to pay their mortgage and other bills. It's frustrating to work on a job for thirty long years just to pay a mortgage. To other people, working is all about vacations and paying bills and eventually retiring and living on their pension. They think that with the pension money they will enjoy more holidays and have more fun, but many eventually get bored and end up in an old people's home or die shortly after retirement. That sounds not so exciting to me.

There is more to life than this type of lifecycle. Too many people work all their lives patiently counting the years to retirement. Some people negotiate early retirement. The fact that people negotiate for early retirement simply tells the whole story that such people were not enjoying their job. Anyone who enjoys what he or she is doing do not want to retire early. That is why some professors remain active even after retirement from classroom teaching. They are called professor emeritus and become consultants or visiting professors.

Getting more out of life is not in making so much money but in doing what you like doing. Doing what you like produces the enthusiasm required to get the job done. The enthusiasm you bring into your job because you love it creates the wealth you desire. Performing your job with enthusiasm makes you a satisfied person, resulting in being a successful person.

The reason why many people are stuck with a job they hate is because of the genuine fear of being unemployed. Similarly, dependence on government hand-outs or benefits is not the only other option. The best option is when you do what you love doing. It may be voluntary work with no salary. If you love it so much that you do it with zeal and passion, it will provide you with all the resources you need to carry on and to have a better life.

Many people have lived much below what life has on offer because they have not reached down within themselves to discover what gives them joy and fulfilment. Doing what you love doing gives you joy and satisfaction, even if you are not paid.

In whatever level of life you are now, there is a better life—there is potential. Whatever you are earning at your current job, there is the potential to earn more. If you are renting a home, there is the potential to own a home. If you are unmarried, there is the potential to build a relationship and eventually marry. If you are struggling with debt, there is the potential to find a way to pay your bills. If you do not like your job, there is the potential to work at something you like to do. There is always a better life awaiting you.

You will never change what you tolerate.

The ability to move from where you are presently to the next better level of life lies within you. This statement seems easier said than done, but the statement is true. Some people will never change their situation for the better because they don't believe they have the ability to change their lives. They have accepted their condition as it is and are just getting by. Until you dislike your present condition and desire to change it for the better, things will remain the same. You can never change what you tolerate. To change your condition you must first of all change your personal philosophy. To change your life, you must start by changing your person. You must change your thinking and have a vision for the life you desire. You must begin to visualize your future—what kind of life you would like to have? It all starts with the choices you make.

John Iroh

Life Is All About Choices

The following is a serious of well-known quotes and variations cited many times over many years—they continue to ring true today: A person is a sum total of the choices he or she makes. A man's choice will either make him or break him. Every choice emanates from a thought process. The mind is the playing field for different kinds of thought. The mind can be likened to an open fertile field; whatever seed that is planted in the field flourishes, be it good seed or bad seed. A person's mind is always besieged with different thoughts hovering over it seeking for attention. We may not be in control of the thoughts that pop into our minds, but we are definitely in control of the thoughts we give attention to and entertain. Thoughts are like seeds and the fruits are the actions that result from our thought process. People are products of their thoughts. As a man thinks in his heart, so is he, is an ancient truth recorded in the Bible.

A person naturally responds in line with and according to his or her pattern of thinking. For instance, a man who rapes a young girl is a result of his meditating on that thought for a considerable time. Likewise, a man who invents children's car seat safety equipment is the result of the man's thought on that subject for a considerable time. The choice is ours.

We can fill our minds with thoughts of kindness and goodness, or we can fill our minds with wicked, evil thoughts. What we allow ourselves to think about is the difference between a criminal and a Sunday school teacher.

The thoughts we harbor or meditate upon determine what and who we are and become.

You are the product of your thoughts.
If you change your thought pattern, you change yourself.

It is almost impossible to equally harbor good thoughts and bad thoughts at the same time. We must choose to allow one to dominate the other and our body will naturally show external expression to the dominating thought. For instance, if there is a thought of serving in a local church choir and a thought of joining a gang, the choice depends on the dominating thought.

By nature, humans are supposed to be able to control their thoughts; however, there are cases where a human loses the control of his or her thought process. In that case, the person is said to be addicted to a particular condition that controls the thought pattern. This happens when the particular thought takes up permanent residence in the person's mind. The person then dwells on the thought instead of the thought dwelling in the person. It is sad when a person loses the power to control what thoughts to entertain in his or her mind. A person who has lost the power of the thought process has lost the power of the mind and power over his or her actions. The person becomes a slave to the dominating thought. Such a person loses the power to be rational and needs help as the thought process becomes subconscious. That is the reason such a person can go to any length to satisfy the desire of such a controlling thought.

An example of this situation is when a man or a woman is in love, or let me say infatuated, with a person of the opposite sex. The person can go to any length, even death to try to express the content of the thought process. Another instance is when someone is addicted to a drug; the person can sell every possession just to satisfy the desire to get the drug. These examples show you the power of the thought process. It propels people into action; be it positive action or negative action. Thought process is the root from which habit is formed. Habit is the foundation for character. Character determines the destiny of a person. Every thought in a person's mind will naturally seek external expression by way of action to reflect the content. The thought we brood upon in our minds determines how we dress, the associations we keep, and even our choice of language.

Parents, teachers, and churches help us from childhood to direct our minds to think correctly. They advise us on what we should and should not watch on television and the Internet. Their advice helps shape our thought patterns. They help to build our character. We grow up to be in control of what thoughts we choose to harbor in our minds and ultimately the choices we make in life.

Plans and Goals

Life generally is all about the choices we make. The choice of what to eat, what clothes to wear, what friends to associate with, what to study in school, who to marry, how many children to have, etc. As a matter of fact, the challenge of choice starts from the moment we awaken in the morning to the time we fall asleep at night. The difference between the achiever, who stands out in the crowd, and the ordinary person is the choices each makes daily. The achiever does not make hasty, reckless, impromptu choices. Achievers have each day pre-planned far ahead so they know exactly the right choice to make when the time comes. Achievers make choices that align to their planned goals and targets.

On the other hand, ordinary people have no plans or goals, so they make thoughtless choices on the spot and accept or deny the consequences of their poor choices. Some consequences of a poor choice may be very unpleasant. Every choice has a consequence. No choice is neutral. Choice obeys the natural law of cause and effect. One wrong choice can result in a consequence that can lead to forever regret. Many of the young people involved in crime that landed them into life in jail or long-term jail sentences were a result of the wrong choices they made. Youths with promising futures sometimes end up living their lives incarcerated because of wrong choices.

To avoid unpleasant consequences as a result of wrong choices, there is the need to have every day planned before the day comes. This helps keep you focused and avoids silly and wrong choices. It also helps in time management. Having your day pre-planned means that you have set for yourself tasks or targets for the day. The tasks and targets are normally based on long-term or short-term goals. Working on set tasks and targets will normally create some excitement as you look forward toward moving closer to your goal.

When there is need for a decision or a choice to be made, it will be made based on your set goals, and you can't go wrong. You are not tossed to and fro, because you already have a plan. So when friends say, "Come join us; let's hang out," you can politely say, "Thank you, but I need to finish this task, then I may join you later." Goals keep you focused. Having a focus is the difference between the person who stands out in the crowd and the ordinary person. There are a lot of good books on setting goals and making plans that work. I encourage you to read such good books to help you set worthwhile goals and put some organization into your thought process.

To achieve intelligent accomplishments, thought must be linked with purpose; otherwise, there is the possibility of making choices that will lead to undesired consequences. People who have discovered a central purpose for their lives will keep their thoughts focused on this purpose. They will refuse to entertain other distracting thoughts seeking attention.

The ultimate purpose of a person provides enough material to meditate upon to keep him or her focused. The thoughts and meditation focuses on the plan or the pathway to achieve the purpose. A person who cannot see the ultimate purpose of his or her life will become a slave to the immediate needs of making daily living. It is sad to note that many people are slaves to seeking the provision of their daily needs. It's disheartening that people go to work just because they need to pay the bills and not because the job is a pathway to achieving their ultimate purpose. Some people pretend to be disabled just to receive government disability funds. There is no purpose to their lives. Their major objective is to pay bills and buy food.

> *You must see the ultimate purpose of your life or you will become a slave to the immediate needs of daily living.*

Thought process is a form of energy. It begins with an idea, which may be just a simple one. If we give the idea some attention and allow it to dominate our thought process, the idea soon grows into some form of energy that propels and channels our actions. Harvesting the energy in these thoughts naturally transforms them into a propelling creative force that influences every decision or choice. A person with purpose backed by this propelling creative force is unstoppable in the things he or she has determined to achieve.

We have to be careful, therefore, what thoughts we allow to dominate our minds and to propel us into action. Positive thoughts propel us into positive actions, while negative thoughts propel us into negative actions. The internal thoughts of our minds provide the energy for external actions, be they negative or positive. Once the thought we inhabit in our minds builds enough energy, it permeates our subconscious and will naturally seek to be released. It is released by our acting out the contents of the thoughts.

Thought Energy

Sometimes the thought energy is so strong that all we want to do is to release it through action. It is only after the release of some of these thought energies that we realize that the resulting actions were negative; and regret follows. That is why it is important that we train our conscious minds to entertain thoughts that will lead to positive outcomes, such as success, happiness, prosperity, and good health. We have to be diligent in monitoring our thoughts by learning to dispose of negative thoughts that pop into our minds before the negative thought traps us.

I believe we can use the resources of our thought energy to our advantage. It is true that we attract what we focus on and believe in. We can consciously choose to establish a working relationship with our minds by partnering with our minds in our pursuit of success. We can utilize the power of our minds to help us achieve our goals and desires. In this mind-partnership, we plant in our minds the thoughts of what we wish to see ourselves become. We plant thoughts of success and great accomplishments. Our role in this partnership with our minds is that we nourish and nurture the thought we plant in our minds by dwelling on the thought and believing in the reality of the thought.

When we dwell on the thoughts, it gradually permeates our subconscious mind and begins to propel us to express the thoughts by our actions. We will naturally attract all of the resources we need to accomplish or release the thought energy that has been formed in us. People of like minds will be more than likely to partner with men and women with a vision. People will put together all the resources you need to achieve your worthwhile purpose. In helping you achieve your dream, they are also fulfilling their own dreams.

A Culture of Positive Change

I have seen this happen in the multilevel marketing (MLM) system. MLM is an idea created by someone to achieve a financial pinnacle while taking many other people along up the success ladder. It's a single idea that was nourished in the thought process, became a subconscious thought, and propelled the originator into action. Today, many people earn a seven-figure income because of this single idea and the choice to act on that idea.

It is the choice to act on our ideas that is important. Some people choose to suppress their ideas when it becomes a propelling force. Some choose to see excuses, not reasons, why it won't work. Some procrastinate even as the thoughts keep popping into the mind seeking expression. Some great dreams have been killed because someone did not act out the good thoughts, or instead, gave attention to the wrong thoughts. To succeed in life is a choice.

Choose to succeed.

2

It All Begins with a Dream

I believe we live in a dreamer's world. Dreamers rule the world. Dreamers are the pacesetters of the world. Dreamers lead the way. Dreamers shape history.

There are many definitions of dream. However, the dream I am referring to is the dream you have for your tomorrow. I refer to your aspirations, goals, aims, objectives, and all the visions you hold in your mind for your desired future and destiny.

Donald Trump, an American entrepreneur, visited Scotland. While in the coastal city of Aberdeenshire, he saw the beauty of the natural landscape by the seaside—an 800-acre stretch of stunning sand dunes. He immediately realized that the site would be good to locate his dream golf village. The following is a quote from Donald Trump:

> When I saw this piece of land I was overwhelmed by the imposing dunes and rugged Aberdeenshire coastline. I knew that this was the perfect site for Trump International, Scotland. I have never seen such an unspoilt

> and dramatic sea side landscape and the location makes it perfect for our development. Our site is close to two of the world's most famous courses and is just 15 minutes by car from Aberdeen International Airport. As this exciting development comes to fruition, the standards for the golf experience in Scotland will be taken to new levels of excellence by the addition of Trump International Golf Links.[1]

Donald Trump had a wonderful dream of a golf village in Europe and spent five years looking for the perfect site. His dream was to make the golf resort the best in the world. To visualize his dream, he transformed the natural landscape of the site into an amazing golf village by putting his dreams on paper in the form of a development master plan and also had models of the plan created. In the beginning, he visualized his dream in his mind, then to see how the finished product would look, he crafted a master plan. The master plan is also the vehicle to communicate his dream to others. Today, the dream—Trump International Golf Links—has become a reality.

The transformations in every industry we see in the world today are due to the collective effort of dreamers. Some of the dreams were labeled as crazy and unachievable. Yet the dreamers continued their quest to create, and the world is better for their tenaciousness.

When I was a kid, my dream was to become a pediatrician. In seeking admission to a university, I followed after my childhood dream. I took the examination to study medicine at the university. However, due to the high competitive nature of the course, my score fell a little below the cut-off score. I took the exam one more time and the same thing happened. Other things happened that resulted in my dropping my dream to study medicine. Instead, I chose to study engineering. It was very sad for me to let go of biology, as it was one of my best subjects. I replaced biology with mathematics in my desire to pass the university exam to study engineering. The competition to study engineering was not as tough as medicine, so I passed my first exam and was admitted to the engineering program.

You may be thinking, *He didn't follow through on his childhood dream.* Yes that's correct, but dreams are not cast in stone. Dreams may be vague at the onset, and then get better defined with time. Nature has a way of aligning us into our perfect place in life—if we continue to follow after our dream. It's all about putting the square peg in a square hole or a round peg in a round hole. Shortly after beginning my engineering courses at the university, I understood why I was falling short of the cut-off score for the school of medicine—my real skills and talents were in the engineering field. I was so glad that I didn't study medicine. I realized that I would have been frustrated if I had followed my infancy dream to study medicine—it just wasn't where I belonged. The supernatural infinite intelligence, who knows my ability, fixed me into my rightful place. I look back today and am so thankful that I studied engineering.

Many people in the world today may have a similar story. For some people, in the process of following after their dream, they received insight that established them for life. Do not be afraid to have a dream. Do not be afraid to dream big. How to achieve your dream may not be clear in the beginning, but as you keep your dream alive by meditating on it, the plans of action will begin to come to you. With time, the dream becomes more defined and more feasible.

Three Types of Dreamers

I have classified dreamers into three categories. There are those who are professional dreamers and stop at that. They have very good dreams and even plans of action, but never follow after their dreams. These people have fantastic ideas of what they plan to do, but they never get around doing those things. These are the people who later complain that their friend stole their ideas. These people complain that someone stole their song. These people procrastinate and seldom make progress in life. They never live to their full potential.

The second category is non-dreamers who believe that "what will be, will be." This set of people has placed their fate into whatever circumstance befalls them. They have no dreams. They have no aspirations. They are tossed to and fro depending on their most recent circumstance. I believe this is a dangerous place to be. People in this category are always looking to someone for help. They depend on the government or charity for some form of support. Their lives are dictated and controlled by others.

The last group of people are those who dare to dream. They are those who see opportunity in challenges. A hotel owner one day saw a dirty glass cup, which gave him the idea of mass producing paper cups. This idea solved his financial needs for life. Dreamers write their own tickets in life. This group of people are the ones who come up with the so-called "crazy" ideas.

Richard Branson is about to commence commercial flight that will take paying customers into suborbital space. That was at first a "crazy" idea, but since he expressed his idea, there have been many people who want to take advantage of the opportunity to see the earth from space. What used to be the exclusive privilege of astronauts is now to be made available to ordinary people because of one man's "crazy" idea. When the idea of a metal object flying in the air was first thought out, people discarded the idea as crazy and utterly impossible. Today, metal objects fly in the airspace every day to and from every country around the world. That crazy idea has changed world transportation. Every invention the world has ever seen came from a dreamer. Alexander Graham Bell's crazy idea of transporting sound through wires has developed into transferring sound through air waves using wireless technology.

I have mentioned these three groups to help you decide which group you would like to fit into. Most kids have dreams about what they would like to become as they grow older. However, most of these childhood dreams are never fully realized by many. A man once told me that he had great childhood dreams and ambition about what he would like to become, but never was. This man lost his dream to the pressure of seeking a daily living. He was caught up in the rat race and lost his childhood dream. Dreams are not wishful desires. They are the foundation of all accomplishment.

A Culture of Positive Change

Dreams are like a fetus growing in the womb. It needs to be nourished and kept alive. It's possible for dreams to be aborted prematurely. When you are pregnant with a dream, nourish it and keep it healthy. As the dream develops, it becomes clearer how to execute it. Discuss it with like-minded people and never discuss your dreams with dream-killers. Ideas will come to you on how to make your dream a reality. If it's so big that you need other people to help execute it, then carefully recruit those who are motivated to see it happen. Keep your dream before you always. Work your dream and talk your dream. The support you need will come if you persevere. Soon you will find that you are among the dreamers who have changed the face of the earth.

Work Your Dream and Talk Your Dream

Maybe at this point you are wondering if you have a dream—or if you *ever* had a dream. Perhaps you never really gave it a thought because you are in your comfort zone, benefiting from some form of charity or government support. Maybe you have just given in to a life of dependency. Or perhaps you are working and hoping that your retirement comes early so you get to stay at home and receive your pension check every month. There is much more to life than what you have now.

You can move up to a better life by acknowledging and fulfilling your dream. If your dream is to join the list of legends who have made the world a better place, then look at the problems confronting the world and seek to be part of the solution. I have a dream that someday vehicles will be installed with external pressure bags that would be sensor-controlled to reduce the effects of vehicle impact with another object. This dream when realized would save lives in the case of accidents.

If your dream is to make additional money to provide a better life for your family, then be willing to look at the many opportunities that exist. The Harry Potter Series of books has made the author, J.K. Rowling, a worldwide phenomenon. The series has solved her financial needs for life. I believe that anybody can write a book, because everybody has a story to tell. You may want to start with a biography. The Internet provides numerous opportunities to create wealth. It brings you into the world market. Owners of Websites like Facebook, YouTube, Google, Wikipedia, and others can testify that the Internet has changed their lives forever. You may find a niche in your local area and use the Internet as leverage. Whatever your desire is in life, dream your way to it.

There Is a Purpose

A vehicle is manufactured for the purpose of transporting people, animals, and materials from one place to another on the road. An airplane is manufactured to fly in the air, over all the obstacles on the ground that affects the movement of cars. Imagine that a person does not understand that the plane is designed to fly in the air and decides to drive it on the ground on its tires like a car. Using an airplane in that manner would amount to an enormous waste of potential and resources. We need to realize our potential and resources and use them to the fullest.

A Culture of Positive Change

A story is told of a man who snatched an eagle's egg from a nest at the top of a mountain. Desperate to hatch an eaglet, the man placed the eagle egg among the eggs of his brooding hen. The hen brooded over the eggs and eventually hatched the eggs including an eaglet. The eaglet, not knowing that it is an eaglet, walked on land and ate what the chickens ate. One day, the eaglet was fascinated seeing birds flying in the sky and it began to separate itself from the chickens. After much gazing into the sky, watching other birds fly and soar in the air, the young eagle flapped its wings and discovered something amazing; it could also fly. Finally, after trying flying every day by flapping its wings, the young eagle finally flew away to where it belonged; far above the chicken coop. The young eagle finally discovered its purpose and rightful place.

There is a definite purpose and plan for the car, the airplane, and the eagle. There is also a definite purpose for every man and woman on the face of the earth. Every person's purpose for existence is unique. The problem is that many individuals do not understand this fact and so most who should be flying like the eagle and the airplane are instead walking around like chicken. There is a purpose for every person and for most events that happen around us. There is even a purpose for challenges that come our way. Challenges are catalysts for new discoveries. Challenges help us take the next step up the ladder of progress.

Everything, including death, has a purpose. The purpose of death is to terminate life after we have achieved our purpose here on earth. It is therefore tragic to die without fulfilling or delivering our purpose. It is painful when someone at the point of death still has unfulfilled dreams and visions. Some of those dreams and visions (purpose) are unique and specific to the individual. That means the visions and dreams will die forever with the person who did not fulfill them. Imagine someone whose destiny lies in discovering the cure for HIV/AIDS, yet never did. People will continue to die of HIV/AIDS because one person did not use the idea deposited in his or her mind to discover the cure. Many discoveries have been deposited in people's minds and are waiting to be brought into existence. Some of these great discoveries may never see the light of the day and die with the carriers. The death of someone full of unaccomplished dreams and visions is agonizing.

As you know, the whole world is trying to find a cure for the HIV disease. I believe someone has the cure as his or her destiny to discover. Hopefully very soon the whole world will celebrate that person because he or she has achieved the purpose that will positively affect the whole of humankind. Someone's purpose was to discover how a heavy metal object could fly in the air against the natural law of gravity. The invention of the airplane revolutionized the world transportation system. The discovery of the Internet has made the world a global village. For one moment, imagine if these people with these purposes were careless and did not fulfill their purposes. Imagine if they had died without delivering their purpose. These purposes would have died and would have been buried with them.

As a matter of fact, there are lots of purposes that never saw the light of the day because the individuals who were supposed to give life to the purposes never did, they died with the dormant purposes still within them. Some people who were meant to be professors with major scientific discoveries to their names died as illiterates. Some others who were to be great philanthropists helping the poor and contributing to orphanages, died in penury. Some who were to be great world evangelists died in prison serving life sentences for heinous crimes. There are men and women with the purpose and abilities of being great musicians, great athletes, and great leaders but ended up in rehab centers. The whole world is full of people with wasted potential, which is so sad. Imagine if the young eagle never discovered that it was an eagle, it would still be pecking around on the ground looking for chicken feed.

The Reason for Our Being

Purpose is the reason for our being; the essence of our existence. Purpose is what gives meaning to our being. Life therefore seems empty without purpose. Purpose gives direction and focus to our lives. Without purpose for living, we are tossed to and fro by every political, social, and economic change. There is indeed no direction in life without purpose. Without purpose, we are preoccupied with working for our daily need for survival. A life with purpose looks at the big picture beyond just putting food on the table.

Purpose for living removes depression and the desire to give up in life through suicide. Depression comes into people's lives when they are disappointed with expectations. Without a purpose-driven life, people allow someone else like the government, a rich uncle, or others to dictate the outcome of their lives. Frustration and depression comes when these external influences disappoints expectations. Purpose puts people in charge of their lives. A purpose-driven life is not moved by temporary defeat. A person with a purpose in life never gives up. This is because purpose provides the inner enthusiasm needed to progress through the challenges of life.

Everyone's purpose stares at them. A person's country and birth family is determined by that person's purpose. Consider the legendary Nelson Mandela, South Africa's first black president. He was born into the apartheid regime of South Africa. Each time he saw the oppression of his fellow citizens, his purpose for existence was stirred up. For twenty years he actively sought to achieve his purpose, risking his life in the process. Today he is a world phenomenon because he answered the call of his purpose. He is celebrated all around the world for his bravery and commitment to help his people. Imagine if Nelson Mandela did not answer the call to achieve his purpose—South Africa may still be under apartheid oppression, and he would not be known beyond his village.

There are many people who see things that stir up a desire in them to change the situation—but many don't respond. You were born in a specific location so you could possibly change a particular situation that makes you sad each time you see it. That is why I say that challenges are not to crush us but to direct us to our purpose. Challenges in life help to bring out the hidden giant that lies dormant inside us. That is the purpose for challenges—to make us realize who we really are, and not to crush us. Therefore, discover the way to overcome your challenges of life.

Imagine someone told you that you can't cope in your studies for whatever reason or excuse. That is a challenge that calls for a positive reaction, not for negative self-pity. Use that statement as a good reason to tell yourself that you are going to work so hard until you become the best in your class. Watch out! That may be the way your journey into your purpose commences. Beyond being the best in your class, you may also find out that you have become an inventor. If you give up and drop out of school because of what someone says, that may be when the path to your destiny is abandoned, or aborted. It could also mean that you have given up your purpose of being a professor with many invention patents to your name or a musician who write beautiful music that soothes a mother's cry.

Many purposes go unaccomplished because someone gave up and gave in to a challenge. In every challenge, there is a positive aspect. Look for that positive aspect in the challenge. It may be your destiny or purpose staring at you for action. Every scientific discovery or breakthrough has been as a result of challenges that seemed insurmountable at the time. Breakthrough happens when people persevere long enough to achieve success. In every labor, there is profit.

Supernatural Endowments

Our inherent talents and natural abilities point us toward our purpose. These natural endowments and gifts, if harnessed and utilized, will make us stars and superstars. Every man and women have been supernaturally equipped for a specific purpose. These purposes are linked to who we are and why we are. There are two types of supernatural endowments for our purpose. There is the one that is easily manifested in a person in the form of talent. A person born to be a singer or musician will showcase ability and likeness for music from an early age. There is a natural pull toward music from infancy for the one endowed with musical talents. A soccer player knows from childhood that he or she is gifted in that direction. The same can be said for most artists, writers, and athletes.

There is another type of supernatural endowment that is not easily visible to the external environment but is resident in most people. This type is naturally activated when it meets the reason or a challenge for its expression. For instance, a young couple on holiday met a group of children orphaned by HIV/AIDS and living in a settlement. The passion within this couple was immediately activated and they went into action doing all they could to help the children have better lives. That may be the destiny and purpose for this young couple. Their destiny was only activated when a challenge was encountered. The couple was endowed with compassion for the needy and the suffering. Every person's purpose for living is unique and so also the natural endowment to each person.

Purpose is not selfish.

One thing that underscores purpose for each individual is that purpose is not selfish. More often than not, the purpose for a person's life seeks to improve the life of others. Purpose seeks to make the world a better place for others. Purpose is sustainable. It tends to improve the life of the generations yet unborn. Every purpose achieved leaves an indelible mark for future generations. Thus, being stunningly wealthy is not an end in itself but a means to accomplishing a certain purpose. Having money without purpose is worse than not having money at all.

Andrew Carnegie, known to be the second richest man in history, after John D. Rockefeller, said, "There is no class so pitiably wretched as that which possesses money and nothing else." Henry Ford also advised, "A business that makes nothing but money is a poor business." These men lived out the purpose for their lives and changed the course of history. They had money, but beyond having money, they also identified the purpose for the money that came their way. Many people are busy chasing money without having any purpose for the money when it comes their way. Discover the purpose for the money you desire and money will come to you in great abundance.

Fulfillment in life comes from pursuing your life purpose to accomplish it. It is possible that a person with the natural endowment for being a musician ends up being a medical doctor due to parental influence or choice. It is easy for parents to decide their child's career path. A person with skills for music who becomes a medical doctor will not be completely fulfilled in that profession no matter the success he or she achieves as a medical doctor.

Success, therefore, is not absolute without fulfillment. A teacher in a high school who chose teaching because that was the only available job at the time may struggle in communication with the pupils if he or she is not gifted in that field. Even though such a teacher may be very good in the subject area he or she teaches, yet the person will struggle to pass on that knowledge to the pupils. The teacher will often be frustrated by the silly behavior of the students. The person does not possess the psychology of a teacher. On the other hand, a gifted teacher is a friend to the students even though the teacher may not be very good in the subject area; yet the teacher is able to communicate and connect with the students. A gifted teacher enjoys the job. When we do what we are born to do, there is fulfillment and satisfaction.

Success is not absolute without fulfillment.

A story was told of a man who died at ninety years of age without really achieving something remarkable in life. The man was unhappy with himself because he felt he had wasted his life. He was angry with God. He asked God why He sent him to earth to waste ninety years of his time without a purpose. God told him that there was a purpose to the man's life. God took the man back to when the man was seventeen years of age, and he was walking along a walkway and saw a banana skin littered on the walkway. He removed the banana skin and dropped it into the bin. Shortly after that, a pregnant woman walked by that walkway. God told the man that the pregnant woman would have slipped on the banana skin had he not removed it. God said that the woman and her unborn child would have died if both fell down from the slip. God informed the man that the reason the man was born was to save the life of the woman and her child.

Our purpose for being is not always for the big inventions or skills that attract international recognition. Purpose may be hidden in the daily things we naturally do. Imagine that removing a banana skin from a railway track could save the life of hundreds of people. Someone may be born to do just that as part of the purpose in that person's life. Being a good father to a son and providing the necessary support for the child to grow up to become a scientist may be your purpose. Being a good mother to a daughter and providing the necessary support for the child to grow up to become an honest politician may be your purpose.

Living a good and responsible life is required to discover and fulfill your purpose—no matter how big or small you think it may be.

Endnote

1. Please see http://www.trumpgolfscotland.com.

3

You Already Possess all You Need to Succeed

A fish is hatched possessing all that it needs to swim and to live in the water. It does not require any special training school on swimming. It comes equipped for its purpose of existing and swimming in water. A bird hatches from its egg with all that it needs to fly. It does not require any special flight lessons to understand how to fly in the air, how to glide, how to soar, or how to perch. All these unique aspects are naturally within a bird. A camel has the ability to survive for days without water because of its design to cross sandy deserts where no water exists. This ability is built in the design of the camel. The horse and the donkey have very strong back bones because of their purpose of carrying loads. The dog has a well-developed sense of smell, so has being effectively used to detect banned or smuggled items such as drugs, also to sniff out bombs.

Likewise, we have, as part of our genetic makeup, all that is required to accomplish our purpose. People are born already equipped for their purpose. Our inherent abilities and our environment are naturally aligned for the accomplishment of our purpose and to make us successful. The geographical location, race, color of skin, family, etc. are all naturally designed for the accomplishment of success in a person's life. We do not need any more than what we already possesses in order to be successful in life—except an enhancement of our inherent abilities. This enhancement may be in the form of training to develop the already existing abilities.

People with skills for music do not need a crystal ball to discover their musical talent. Most musical superstars start performing even before they attend school, so it's not from formal education that they succeed. It's part of their genetic make-up. Most actors and actresses discover from an early age that they have special interest and ability in stage performance, so they get involved in church and school drama activities. Comedians have a natural talent to make people laugh, even when they do not intend to cause laughter. Every speech from a comedian has something funny about it. A comedian cannot hide his or her personality. It's all naturally in-built in the comedian.

Inventors naturally preoccupy themselves in their pursuit to invent that they consider every other thing a distraction. Most inventors are not the best in their formal education classes because their minds are preoccupied with the thought of their new invention. The drive for invention is already within them. They are pregnant with their invention. Every successful inventor is someone who discovered his purpose and achieved it. The ability and wisdom to invent is already within the inventor. An inventor expresses who he or she is with an invention.

Every person is born already equipped for his or her purpose.

It is disheartening to note that not every person with the ability to invent becomes an inventor. Most people with the ability to invent do not discover this purpose and some have passed through this earth unnoticed. The world has lost people with great potential who never discovered the greatness in them. They robbed the world of their contribution to make the world a better place. The world has lost many great talents that were never expressed. The world is robbed when a person with the potential of being a university professor dies without even going to college. The world is robbed when someone with the ability of being a great pastor spends most of his life in jail. The world is robbed when a person with the ability of being a wonderful pediatrician turns out to be a pedophile. Great talents and in-built abilities can be wasted if there is no conscious effort to discover the purpose for living.

Many people are pregnant with books that could change lives, but most of these books are never written. People are pregnant with songs and music that would be of great blessing to the generations, but many never write the songs or music. The world is robbed from benefitting from these natural in-built abilities that were never expressed. Every man and woman has a contribution to make in life. Express yourself by living your dream and fulfilling your purpose. There is a role for you in the affairs of this life. Discover your role and fulfill it.

You may wonder, *What are my own abilities?* Or, *What is my purpose?* Or, *What role do I have to play in this life?* The truth is that nobody is born to be ordinary or redundant. Everyone has something to offer. Every person has the in-built potentials to stand out and be counted in history. However, most people do not harness these potential qualities in order to bring them to light. Most people do not care enough to stand out or do not know how to do that. Some are just happy passing through history and not being part of history. Everyone has equal opportunity to stand out, but only those who embrace the natural provisions within and around them will actually stand out. Others that do not, will not.

Every success that a person will ever achieve is already resident in the person from the moment of birth. The success stories of multimillionaires, owners of worldwide corporations, owners of holiday resorts, leaders in medical breakthroughs, pastors who have touched millions with the Good News, and all the great achievements a person can attain were already deposited in these achievers from birth. Achievers are those who work hard with purpose to realize the success that they possess within. Each man and woman is a success waiting to happen. The degree of success people bring out from the success deposited inside them is completely dependent on each person.

You are a success waiting to happen!

Many people never really understand the power that exists within them, and so they live far below their potential. It's like a water pump operating at 10 percent efficiency; it doesn't produce much. Many people live their lives at just about 10 percent capability of what they can actually achieve. Also, many people spend much money studying something different from their real purpose. It takes so much effort and stress when we invest our energy and resources on something different from the real purpose for our lives. People who are in the wrong job or profession will eventually realize that they may be efficient, but never effective. It is like using a large bath towel to wipe your car's side mirror. The towel is efficient, but not effective. More effort is required to clean your car's side mirror using an extra-large towel rather than a paper towel sheet designed to clean small mirrors.

We must not use the right equipment for the wrong purpose. For instance, it would be a waste of resources to use a cannon to catch a rabbit. And there is a knife made specifically for cutting bread just as there is a knife made for cutting meat at the butchery. Using a butcher knife to cut bread may destroy the bread. Similarly, using a bread knife to cut meat would require a lot more effort and time. Understanding who we are and applying our skills and talents on the right jobs will bring fulfillment and eliminate complaints from our lives.

Do not live just to make a living, but live to make an impact in your world. Life with a purpose will always have a positive impact in the family, workplace, neighborhood, and beyond. It is therefore important that we invest our energy in the right purpose for which we are naturally endowed or gifted. I believe that all people are born equal with equal chance of success. No one has an advantage over another notwithstanding the geographical country of birth or family background; notwithstanding the opportunities provided by the family. I have seen people from very poor families with no formal education become great leaders known worldwide. I have also seen privileged people from very wealthy families become public enemies and total failures. That tells me that success lies within each individual.

A successful life is a life guided by purpose. Purpose is achieved by setting goals. Life has no focus without goals. Goals have no meaning without purpose. Purpose is the essence of life—the reason for being. Everyone has, locked within, the purpose for being and the requisite ability to unlock the purpose and accomplish it. Every person who learns to set goals linked toward accomplishing his or her purpose will stand out in history.

Purpose is the essence of life—the reason for being.

Let's take a look at some people who expressed their inherent abilities and made a positive impact in the world. These people stood out not because of adequate education (for some of them never had formal education), not because their families were wealthy, and not because of their geographical location. They were able to harness the potential that lies within every human on the face of the earth. They discovered their purpose and achieved it.

Thomas Edison was a man with a humble beginning who developed a hearing disability at an early age. The cause of his hearing problems were attributed to a bout of scarlet fever during his childhood and recurring untreated middle age infections. Thomas Edison had only three months of formal education as his mind was said to have often wandered and his teacher called him "slow" and that his young brain was scrambled.[1]

The young Edison was quoted as saying, "My mother was the making of me. She was so true, so sure of me; and I felt I have something to live for, someone I must not disappoint."

Thomas had two favorite pastimes—reading and experimenting, with experimenting taking more of his time than reading. He became one of the world's greatest inventors, scientists, and businessman—holding 1,093 United States patents to his name. His name is synonymous with, among other things, the discovery of electric light used in every modern home today. When Edison made the first public demonstration of his incandescent light bulb, he was quoted to have said, "We will make electricity so cheap that only the rich will burn candles." This certainly was the statement of someone who has discovered his purpose in life and was living the purpose.

A person of purpose does not stop at his present achievement but looks instead at the big picture. The big picture is the destiny while the present achievements are the steps toward fulfillment of destiny. Thomas Edison understood that he had something to live for. Even his partial deafness and lack of formal education was not enough to stop him from fulfilling his purpose.

Do not live just to make a living—live to make an impact in your world.

Henry Ford, a friend of Thomas Edison and a one-time chief engineer in Edison Illuminating Company, was the founder of the Ford Motor Company and the father of modern assembly lines used in mass production. Ford had a vision of mass-producing inexpensive automobiles using an assembly line. As the owner of Ford Motor Company, he became one of the richest and best known people in the world. His company became the largest automobile manufacturer worldwide. He realized his dream and stood out in his generation. His secret for accomplishment was his belief in possibility. He was quoted as saying that "Nothing is particularly hard if you divide it into small jobs" and "There is one rule for the industrialist and that is: Make the best quality of goods possible at the lowest cost possible, paying the highest wages possible." He is known to be one of the greatest industrialists in his days. He stood out—and many continue to benefit from the potential he fulfilled.

Self-Imposed Limitations

Henry Ford understood that most of the limitations faced by individuals are self-imposed, which is a grave error. The ability to accomplish great things is already part of our makeup. The ability is already within us. However, our body responds to our thought process. So if we doubt our ability to perform, we perform below our capability. If we think we can't perform, we can't. If we tell ourselves we can do it, we can. Whatever the mind thinks is the result we get externally.

John D. Rockefeller was a boy who had hoped to go to college, but he dropped out of high school to go to work to support his family. While looking for work, rather than going to small companies, he went to the big establishments and eventually got a job as an assistant book keeper at the age of sixteen. He threw himself into the job with missionary intensity. At the age of eighteen, he borrowed one thousand dollars with interest and started his first business in commodity trading. As his earnings grew, his ambition grew likewise. At the age of nineteen, he ventured into oil prospecting. He donated from his first salary about 6 percent of his earnings to charity. This was increased to 10 percent by the time he was age twenty. As his wealth grew, so also was his giving.

By age twenty-five, J.D. Rockefeller's oil refinery was one of the largest in the world. He became the first man in history to make a billion dollars. He had the greatest personal fortune in history; nearly 2 percent of American economy. His fortune was used to create a modern systematic approach of targeted philanthropy. His foundations had and still have a major effect on medicine, education, and scientific research. His foundations pioneered the development of medical research that was instrumental in the eradication of hookworm and yellow fever.

His legacy remains well-known today as most of the major oil companies in operation are offshoots of J.D. Rockefeller's Standard Oil Company, including Chevron, Exxon Mobil, BP, and Amoco.

As a youth, Rockefeller allegedly said that his two great ambitions were to make $100,000 and to live 100 years. He died at 98 years, two years short of his ambition, but his legacy lives on, changing lives for the better.

The story of Andrew Carnegie is unique. He was born into a poor weaver's family in Scotland during hard times with starvation throughout the country. His father

A Culture of Positive Change

immigrated to the United States on borrowed money hoping for a better life. His first job in the United States was as a messenger boy in a telegraph company and he progressed up the ranks. He later established businesses that supplied rails and bridges to the railroad.

After the civil war, Carnegie left the railroads to devote all his energy in the ironworks trade. Carnegie made his fortune in the steel industry, controlling the most extensive integrated iron and steel operations ever owned by an individual in the United States. One of his two great innovations was in the cheap and efficient mass production of steel rails for railroad lines. Carnegie Steel was the largest manufacturer of pig iron, steel rails, and coke in the world. He envisioned an integrated steel industry that would cut costs, lower prices to consumers, produce in greater quantities, and raise wages for workers. To realize this vision, he bought out several major steel producers and integrated them into one corporation. He formed the United States Steel Corporation that became the first corporation in the world with a market capitalization of over $1 billion.[2]

Carnegie believed in using his fortune for the betterment of humankind. He was quoted as saying, "There is no class so pitiably wretched as that which possesses money and nothing else." Andrew Carnegie spent his last years as a philanthropist providing the capital for purposes of public interest and educational advancement.

These people discussed saw opportunities where others saw challenges. They embraced problems as challenges that must be overcome. They did not quit or give up.

They understood the potential that existed inside them. They saw the ability to make wealth as a means to achieving a greater purpose, rather than an end in itself. To these people, money was to serve the purpose of improving the lives of others, which is why they were involved in some form of philanthropy.

Endnotes

1. Please visit the following website for additional information: http://www.thomasedison.com/biography.html.
2. Please visit: http://www.biography.com/people/andrew-carnegie.

4

World-Changers

The world as we know it today would not be as it is without the contributions made by some of the people presented in this chapter. I can say with certainty that the contributions made by them have made the world a better place. I studied the lives of these people to understand what set them apart from the rest. I looked at their childhoods to see if they faced the same type of peer pressure encountered by young people today. I wondered if there were issues of binge drinking and knife crime in times past, as in modern times? Well, before I discuss some of the findings, I present to you some youths whose inventions and ingenuity shaped the world we enjoy today.

Alexander Graham Bell[1]

The world remains grateful to Alexander Bell for his invaluable invention—the telephone. Imagine what the world would be like without the telephone. Bell was quoted as saying that "A man as a general rule owes very little to what he is born with—a man is what he makes of himself." This young man, born in Edinburgh, Scotland, at a time when tuberculosis was ravaging the city, devoted much of his time to experimenting how sound could be transmitted through electric wires. The success of his experiments changed the face of communication in the world forever and we owe him sincere gratitude.

As a young child, Bell was fascinated with sound and experimented with sound waves and speech. He worked extensively in medical research and invented techniques for teaching speech to the deaf. His idea was to teach the deaf to communicate vocally, not using sign language. In this way he was able to communicate with his mother, who progressively became deaf when Bell was twelve years old, by speaking to her on her forehead. Suffice it to say that this area of research is still open to development. I therefore encourage every person reading this book and wondering what he or she can do to contribute positively to the world to embrace and expand upon this research thought of Bell's—that the deaf can be taught to communicate vocally without the use of sign language.

Thomas Telford[2]

Perhaps you may have heard the name Thomas Telford. Put in another way, anyone with some interest in engineering is familiar with the name. The history of engineering development in the world is not complete without the mention of Thomas Telford.

Telford's works are clearly visible all across Europe. Among his works include a canal in the English midlands, canal tunnels in the North Country, the Gota Canal in Sweden, St. Katherine Docks in London, and roads that opened up the Scottish Highlands. It is the opinion of many that Thomas

A Culture of Positive Change

Telford is one Scot who made a difference to countless generations because his work improved highways and bridges, canals and roads, which made much of the Industrial Revolution possible by providing the means of transporting men, machinery, raw materials, and finished goods.

In his native Scotland, Telford constructed the Caledonian Canal that connects the Scottish East Coast at Inverness with the West Coast at Corpach near Fort Williams. This canal opened up the lowlands to industry. Also among the notable works of Thomas Telford are the harbour works at Aberdeen, Dundee, and Peterhead.

Telford's father, a shepherd, died only months after he was born. From childhood, Telford was employed as a stonemason apprentice, occasionally attending the parish school of Westerkirk where his quickness and diligence made up for his lack of opportunity. He very much enjoyed reading and writing. He was largely self-taught and extended his talents learning the basics of construction projects ranging from materials involved to the overall management of building projects. He gained practical experience working at the Portsmouth dockyard and later as surveyor of public works. He completed the Montford stone bridge, which was the first of 40 bridges built in Shropshire and gained him a reputation as one of Britain's greatest engineers. He was later appointed engineer for the Ellesmere Canal which became one of his greatest engineering successes. It involved the construction of the Pontcysyllte Aqueduct supported on piers over 120 feet high and carries the canal over 1,000 feet across the River Dee.

Eventually Telford was elected President of the prestigious Institution of Civil Engineers (ICE) from its foundation.

From the story of his beginning, it becomes clear that Thomas Telford was not as fortunate as most young men of his time (1757-1834) in terms of educational opportunities. Despite his lack of quality, formal education, he excelled internationally. He stretched engineering to its boundary thereby changing the face of modern engineering. It is on record that during his time, he built the longest suspension bridge in the world—the Menai Bridge—that connected the Isle of Anglesey to mainland Wales. Engineering has continued to progress, so the Menai Bridge is not the longest suspension bridge today.

If you are already thinking that engineering has been completely explored and there is nothing left for you to contribute, I would dare say not to reach such a hasty conclusion. As you may know, every challenge brings with it an equal or greater opportunity. There have been reports of earthquakes and floods in some parts of the world. It is high time engineers began designing and building structures that are not just earthquake resistant but structures that can float on water in time of flood. This idea of mine may seem crazy, but I believe it is worthy of consideration. Every great invention seems crazy and unachievable in the beginning. I think that flooding disasters provide a great opportunity for research into building technology that would allow buildings to float, at the same location, on the flood plain and not become submerged. This is just one example revealing engineering grounds yet uncovered.

A Culture of Positive Change

Moving away from engineering, I present to you next an English gentleman who lived many centuries ago—but he and his work are still relevant to the world today and shall continue to be relevant for centuries to come—Sir Isaac Newton.

Sir Isaac Newton[3]

History has it that Sir Isaac Newton (1642-1727) was born premature three months after the death of his father. When Isaac was three years old, his mother remarried and left Isaac to the care of his maternal grandmother. It's easy to understand that young Newton was like any child of his age today because he disliked his step-father and hated his mother for marrying him.

Newton is said to be one of the greatest scientists in recorded history. His discoveries in the field of mathematics, optics, mechanics, and gravitation laid the foundation upon which further scientific discoveries were made. He discovered the three laws that govern motion, which are still taught in science classrooms today.

As a child, Newton was bullied at school, even though he did not get the opportunity to go to school until he was twelve years old. However his curiosity led him to study and to experiment. He is quoted to have said, "To myself I am only a child playing on the beach, while vast oceans of truth lie undiscovered before me."

Newton was reunited with his mother at the age of 12 after his mother's second husband died. After his basic education, his uncle persuaded Newton's mother to have him enter the university. During his first three years at Trinity College in Cambridge, Newton was taught the standard curriculum, but he was fascinated with more advanced science.

It is possible that as you read about these people who fulfilled their potential, you may wonder if the world will ever produce such greatness again. The answer is an emphatic Yes! I believe some of the greatest scientists in the world today are from the United Kingdom (UK) and the United States. Many current medical breakthroughs have been pioneered in the UK; for instance, tissue and organ replacement is well-advanced in the UK. However, there are still many more discoveries to be made in the field.

As you read through these pages, you may be wishing or aspiring to be among those who are changing lives and making the world a better place. If that is your aspiration, then brace yourself for a great journey of discovery. I have also researched what these great personalities have in common. While each person has individual characteristics, there are also the characteristics that every great person shares in common. These common characteristics are discussed throughout the pages of this book, and I encourage you to consider adopting them into your mindset.

Sometime in the late 1800s, there was a growing acceptance that a variety of ailments were caused by bacteria and other microbes. As a result, scientists devoted time and other resources to searching for drugs that would kill these disease-causing bacteria. I introduce to you the

Scottish man who delivered the world from the ravaging attack of disease-causing bacteria—Sir Alexander Fleming.

Sir Alexander Fleming[4]

Sir Alexander Fleming (1881-1955) was born to Scottish parents; but unfortunately, his father died when he was only seven years old. As a student, he was outstanding in his academic performance, which led him to join the research team of Saint Mary's Hospital, in Paddington, London. Having witnessed the death of many soldiers due to infected wounds, Fleming became actively involved in the search for antibacterial agents. His steadfastness was rewarded with his discovery of an antibacterial agent that he named penicillin.

His discovery of the world's first antibiotic or bacteria killer revolutionized the face of medicine in the world. In 1999, *Time Magazine* named Sir Alexander Fleming as one of the most important persons of the 20th century for his discovery of penicillin. This discovery of the wonder antibiotic has saved the lives of many from diseases that previously had no cure. *Time Magazine* stated that "it was a discovery that would change the course of history." His discovery has been very vital in the fight of human scourges such as syphilis and tuberculosis. This Scottish man, Alexander Fleming, was honored with the Noble Prize in Medicine in 1945 for his revolutionary work. Surely Fleming fulfilled his destiny and left his footprints on the sands of time.

Mary Slessor[5]

In citing people who shaped the world or changed the face of the earth, the West African country, Nigeria, will never forget the Scottish woman—Mary Slessor.

Mary Slessor (1848-1915) was born in Aberdeen, Scotland. Her father was a shoemaker who was often drunk. Her mother was a sweet-faced godly woman. At the age of eleven, her family moved to Dundee where Slessor worked in a weaving factory to support her family. She educated herself while on her weaving machine and served God faithfully despite the hardships she faced as a child working twelve hours a day, six days a week. It is believed that this hardship may have helped prepare her for her missionary work in West Africa.

To understand the magnitude of the work that Slessor did in Calabar, a coastal city in Nigeria, I would explain the situation of this city prior to her decision to go to the people of the city to change the situation. Slessor was told several times not to go, considering the enormous danger she faced in wanting to live among these people. But she was determined to help and change these people for good. Now, brace up as I tell you about this city and its people that Slessor was willing to sacrifice her life for in order to bring a positive change to their lives.

When Slessor first arrived in Calabar, she was twenty-eight years of age. It was a turbulent time in the history of that region in Nigeria. The slave trade had just been done away with through the efforts of William Wilberforce causing

A Culture of Positive Change

some political, social, and economic imbalance in Calabar, which had been major slave trade route in coastal Nigeria. Slave trade had actually torn the region apart resulting in severe enmity between rival villages. During the slave trade, it was a common occurrence for rival villages to capture people from neighboring villages and sell them to slave merchants. There were occasional wars between rival villages, sometimes over insignificant misunderstandings such as someone fishing in the neighboring river beyond the assumed boundary.

Witchcraft and superstition was prevalent in the region. Human heads were used to accompany the burial of a village dignitary. It was believed that a village chief or dignitary would also require the service of his wives and house helps in the spirit world; hence, when such a person died, his wives and servants were also killed and buried together with the village chief so they could continue to serve the chief in the spirit world or the land of the dead. Twins were considered evil and were thrown into the evil forest to die or to be eaten by wild animals. The mothers of twins were banished from the village forever.

Also during this time in this region of Nigeria, each family had a shrine that symbolized idol worship. The blood of animals was fed to the idol gods. To show that each family was strong and warlike, human skulls were hung on a hut located in the center of the compound. The skulls were to warn visitors to the compound that the family was a warrior family and should not be taken for granted. Also some families worshiped the skulls of dead men. People lived in constant fear of evil spirits.

This was the situation when Slessor began her missionary work in this coastal region. She was told several times that it was very dangerous to move there alone, but she believed it would be more effective to live among the people she dedicated her life to help. Slessor devoted hers early days to learning the language. Once she could communicate in their language, she began teaching them about the love of Christ. She taught the men to stop killing the wives and the slaves of a "big man" (leader) as they could not help him in the spirit world. She taught them to stop worshiping the skulls of dead men. To a people who did not know what love was, Slessor brought the love of Christ.

Among her achievements in these remote coastal villages was how she replaced intertribal wars with intertribal cultural interaction. She encouraged and brought about local trading and intermarriages among the previously warring villages. She stopped the stoning and killing of perceived witches. Slessor is mostly remembered stopping the killing of twins and the banishing from the village the mother of twins. Slessor, the "wee Scottish girl" embedded herself in the history of Nigeria by changing the culture of a people and introducing a better, less violent way to live. The story of Mary Slessor is taught in every primary school in Nigeria.

Florence Nightingale[6]

Florence Nightingale (1820-1910) is a universally known name. She was a celebrated English nurse who believed that God called her to be a nurse. Her pioneering work in nursing during the Crimean war, where she tended to wounded soldiers, brought her to prominence. She was popularly known as "the lady with the lamp" due to her habit of making rounds at night. In the silent darkness when all the medical officers had retired for the day, Nightingale would be noticed as she walked alone quietly along each corridor, with a little lamp in her hand, making her solitary rounds. She was like a ministering angel as the face of every sick fellow was softened with gratitude at the sight of her. She was present to ease the misery of the sick and suffering.

This young nurse, born to a rich British family, laid the foundation of the modern-day professional nursing, with the establishment of the first secular nursing school in the world at Saint Thomas Hospital in London. The annual International Nurses Day is celebrated around the world on Nightingale's birthday.

Nightingale's decision to become a nurse was strongly opposed by her family; but she stood by her decision, being inspired by what she took as a call from God. She worked hard to educate herself in the science of nursing despite the restrictive societal expectations for an affluent young English woman. She did everything in her power to follow her calling including rejecting courtship by politician and poet Richard Monckton Milnes, 1st Baron Houghton.

History has it that Nightingale mentored Linda Richards; America's first trained nurse who returned to the United States with adequate training and knowledge to establish high-quality nursing schools and later became a great nursing pioneer in the United States and Japan.

Nightingale's lasting contribution in founding the modern nursing profession, is the fact that she set an example of compassion, commitment to patient care, diligence, and thoughtful hospital administration. Her school of nursing continues today as the Florence Nightingale School of Nursing and Midwifery at King's College in London. Worldwide there are many foundations named after Florence Nightingale, the English woman who revolutionized the quality of patient care in medical facilities.

We have so far discussed youths whose activities shaped the modern world. Most of the people we have discussed so far are those who lived many decades ago. History is made every day by those who were fortunate to discover a purpose for their lives and pursue the accomplishment of the purpose with singular focus. Even today, history is still being made. I shall now discuss people who are currently making history by discovering and pursing a purpose for their lives and working to achieve that purpose.

Sir Richard Branson[7]

As a young boy, Sir Richard Branson (1950—) had a poor academic performance because of a learning disability. However, he later discovered his ability to connect with people, which he utilized to build his great fortune. At the age of sixteen, the young English boy had his first successful business venture, publishing a magazine called *Student*.

Then Branson started business trading discounted music cut-out records that he sold from the trunk of his car. He later had enough money to start a music record shop in

A Culture of Positive Change

London from where he launched his Virgin Records label. As his record business grew, he bought a country estate in which he installed a recording studio. His record business was the birth of what is known today as the Virgin Empire or the Virgin Brand.

Businesses in the Virgin Brand include Virgin Atlantic Airways, Virgin Mobile (Media), Virgin Blue (Australia), Virgin Trains, Virgin Express, Virgin Nigeria, and Virgin America. These Virgin Brand businesses are known for their world-class service delivery. The Virgin Brand has provided employment for thousands of families and also has positively affected global economy. This was the dream of an English boy who did not allow a learning difficulty to overshadow his ability to connect with people. Branson discovered this asset that he possessed and utilized it to become a global success. He wrote in his autobiography, "My interest in life comes from setting myself huge, apparently unachievable challenges and trying to rise above them."

In the spirit of conquering apparent unachievable challenges, Branson signed a deal under which his tourism company, Virgin Galactic, will take passengers into suborbital space. The Virgin Brand, Virgin Galactic, will make flights available to the public to view the earth from suborbital space. This thrill was previously experienced only by astronauts; but Branson plans to make an out-of-this-world experience available to anyone willing to pay the price.

Branson also has a goal to improve the earth's environment. For this reason, he has pledged to invest profit from Virgin Atlantic and Virgin Trains to help solve global warming by seeking an environmentally friendly fuel. This project will be driven by the Virgin Brand—Virgin Fuels. Branson is involved in numerous other humanitarian initiatives aimed at making the earth a better place to live and improving the lives of those who inhabit it. Branson is another amazing story of a young English boy who has contributed enormously to better the lives of other people by his ability to think outside the box and exercise his creative instinct. He is quoted as saying, "A business has to be involving, it has to be fun, and it has to exercise your creative instincts."

Today, the Virgin Group employs tens of thousands of tax-paying employees.

Simon Cowell[8]

Simon Cowell (1959—) became popular for his brutally honest and blunt remarks to contestants in his role as judge in the talent hunt television programs, "American Idol," "The X-Factor," and "Britain's Got Talent." Many view Cowell as a notorious judge for his often controversial criticisms and insults to the contestants. The contestants dread Cowell more than the other judges and try their best to get a positive response from him for their performance.

Cowell dropped out of school at the age of sixteen. He started his career working as a mail deliverer at EMI and eventually worked his way up the career ladder to become an Artists and Repertoire (A&R) representative. Cowell later founded Syco, a trading name for Simco limited that operates under the Sony Music banner. Syco TV produces talent shows such as "The X-Factor." Syco Music signs the winners and other outstanding artists.

Crowell's roles as an A&R executive, television producer, and a talent show judge has resulted in the discovery and the establishment of talents that may never have had the opportunity to see the light of the day. He has helped many people discover their talent and also helped them step into the international limelight. His role in these talent hunt TV programs challenges people who believe they possess talents to showcase such talents. His signature program, "The X-Factor," produces at least one star each year it runs.

* * *

I have presented briefly some people who have left legacies and some who are making history. Every country has produced such people who have chosen to follow their dreams and fulfill their potential. Others who come quickly to mind and who have influenced the world include William Shakespeare, William Wilberforce, Isambard K. Brunel, Michael Faraday, Stephen Hawking, and David Beckham. They discovered the purpose for their lives and walked through all the youthful challenges to accomplish their dreams. Today they are world celebrities.

There are too many people who wallow into oblivion because they succumb to youthful pressure or have been swallowed in the distractions that life presents. Each of us has a choice to make—to succeed and be celebrated or to follow the majority who go through life unnoticed.

For those who decide to follow their dreams and succeed in accomplishing their dreams, they will never regret fulfilling their destinies.

Next you will learn about the common traits of successful people, as I have learned from studying them.

Endnotes

1. http://www.biography.com/people/alexander-graham-bell.
2. http://www.ice.org.uk/About-ICE/Who-we-are/Our-history; http://www.history.co.uk/biographies/thomas-telford.
3. http://www.newton.ac.uk/newtlife.html; http://newton.ac.uk/newton.html; http://www.biography.com/people/isaac-newton-9422656.
4. http://www.bbc.co.uk/history/historic_figures/fleming_alexander.shtml.
5. http://maryslessor.org/mary-slessor; http://www.truthfulwords.org/biography/slessortw.html; http://www.leisureandculturedundee.com/library/slessor.
6. http://www.bbc.co.uk/history/historic_figures/nightingale_florence.shtml; http://www.bbc.co.uk/schools/primaryhistory/famousepeople/florence_nightingale.
7. http://www.biography.com/people/richard-branson-9224520.
8. http://en.wikipedia.org/wiki/Simon_Cowell.

5

Common Traits of Successful People

In studying well-knowns from Great Britain who changed the world, I have observed some common denominators that I share with you in this chapter. These common denominators are principles that all successful people have adhered to on the road to greatness. If you want to stand out from the crowd, I encourage you to adopt these five vital principles: purpose, passion, perspective, education, and self-confidence.

Purpose

It is difficult to achieve any form of success without a purpose. These great personalities were able to achieve high levels of success because they discovered a purpose for their existence. Discovery of the purpose for your life helps you maintain focus and concentrate every effort toward the fulfilment of that purpose. The foundation of a meaningful life is the discovery of purpose for your life. Florence Nightingale discovered as a teenager that she was born to be a nurse. Her decision to find a career in medicine was opposed by her rich parents who wanted her to marry one of the wealthy and influential suitors who were trying to entice her. She was convinced that her purpose in life was to be a nurse and so refused to marry any of the suitors who would derail her plans to achieve her purpose. It may suffice to say that had Nightingale married and not become a nurse, she may never have been known in history. Fortunately for the world, she was focused on her purpose and concentrated all her energy toward accomplishing it. Today she is still known worldwide—decades after her death.

For anyone wishing to live a meaningful and successful life, it helps to define a direction for your life toward a destination of your choice. The destination would be a sum total of what you would want your life to be. Andrew Carnegie, the Scottish-born industrialist and one-time richest man in the world, was quoted as saying, "The men who have succeeded are men who have chosen one line and stuck to it." This quote simply means that people who have succeeded are those who were focused on the pursuits of their endeavor, refusing to be distracted in any form. Purpose is directional.

Passion

Passion is the driving force; the compelling emotion or the enthusiasm behind a successful outcome. Every one of the great personalities I mentioned had a passion for the job that made them world-renown. David Beckham, famous soccer player, said in an interview, "At school whenever the teachers asked, 'What do you want to do when you're older?' I'd say, 'I want to be a soccer player.' And they'd say, 'No, what do you really want to do . . . for a job?' But that was the only thing I ever wanted to do."

The passion for what you are born to do will give you singularity of purpose. Passion for the job you do keeps you walking and working through any challenge until you succeed. Passion to provide electric light in a bulb led Thomas Edison to conduct about ten thousand experiments before success. Each failure provided vital knowledge toward success. He did not give up, because he had the propelling force called passion. He did not accept failure, rather he was excited at discovering ways that the experiment didn't work. Finally Edison discovered that *one* way the experiment worked. His passion is the reason we can enjoy light in our homes and offices today.

The passion Florence Nightingale had for nursing was so strong that she believed marriage to prominent suitors would interfere with her calling. Have you ever read an interesting novel that kept you awake all night until you read the last page? Or have you read a novel that made you lock your door and refuse to answer the telephone because you did not want any distractions until you read through the novel? That is what passion does. Passion will keep hunger away from you until you achieve success. It is the passion for the profession that keeps wrestlers going back into the ring despite the broken bones or torn muscles they suffer. You may succeed in a career with just hard work and no passion, but the addition of passion makes you to stand out in your career.

Perspective

One important principle applied by every great man or woman is that he or she focuses on the big picture of their pursuit or endeavor. Their focus is on how the achievement of their purpose will benefit the society. Most of these great personalities consider how their effort will improve society—not how their effort will bring them money and fame. Inevitably, money and fame come as by-products, but that is not the major reason for all the hard work.

Sir Alexander Fleming slept in the laboratory and worked day and night until he discovered penicillin, the antibiotic. His primary focus was to save the world from the bacteria epidemic. Florence Nightingale gave up her comfort in order to teach the world how to provide better nursing services and changed the nursing profession. Simon Cowell is helping discover talents that may otherwise not have seen the light of day. He is helping individuals discover their talents and fulfill their dreams. Richard Branson is sponsoring research and activities to make this world a better place.

It is difficult to be counted as successful if the success does not improve other people's lives. Your perspective must be bigger than yourself. It is not selfish. It is not all about money. It is about the lives you improve. Your purpose in life must improve lives if you are to be counted among the great.

Education: Not a Prerequisite

While formal education may be necessary to develop inherent skills and abilities, it is never a pre-requirement for success. It is believed by some that formal education places people at a greater advantage in becoming successful in life. I personally do not believe in that dogma, because most of the great inventors, scientists, athletes, artists, and other great personalities did not have a good, formal education. This is not to say that education is not important, but that success in life is not dependent on formal education.

Education does not give someone the ability to play football or soccer, it can only develop the skills already present in the person. I believe that every person has some unique skills and abilities that are inherent—part of the person's make up. Education may help to develop those skills and abilities. The path to greatness begins when someone discovers his or her inherent abilities or talents. This is why I love "The X-Factor" and "Britain's Got Talent" and similar talent-hunt projects. These programs help people discover and develop their inherent talents. You may never attend a university, and yet you may become a great personality by discovering and developing your talent.

Confidence

This principle is one of the most important principles I have discovered in every great achiever—confidence. All the people discussed and other great achievers believed in their ability to achieve what they set out to achieve. The great British engineer, Brunel believed he was able to design and construct the longest suspension bridge in the world. Florence Nightingale believed she had something to contribute to the medical profession that would revolutionize modern medical practice. Alexander Fleming believed he had the ability to discover the anti-bacteria drug, penicillin, which changed the field of medicine.

Without belief in yourself; without confidence, there is hardly any achievement. You, the achiever, must first believe that you are able to accomplish the undertaking you have set out to accomplish. Belief in your abilities and talents is crucial in achieving success. Anything to the contrary only leads to failure. Belief and passion are directly related, as passion compels belief. However, it is possible for belief to exist without the passion to drive it. For great achievement, the two must coexist.

6

Has Anything Changed?

You may be wondering if every discovery has been done and there is nothing more to discover. Or perhaps you may even think that the world has changed so much that opportunities to make a difference are limited compared to the past few decades. Indeed the world has moved on. The world has moved from discovery of laws of motion to the application of laws of motion. The world has moved from the amazing discovery that sound could travel through wires to the world of wireless communication. The world has moved from the discovery of antibiotic to the wonders of stem cells treatment. Yes, things have changed; but the opportunities for creativity, invention, and discovery exist with every generation. There is much more out there crying for discovery.

All changes come with challenges. Information technology and the Internet have made the world a global village. Barriers in communication due to distance have been broken. It is now possible to have a conference meeting with people in other continents of the world, yet as if all the people are in the same room. These days, seminar organizers do not need to hire large conference rooms for their seminars. All that is required is to give seminar attendees online access to the virtual conference room. The good thing is that anybody from any part of the world can attend an online seminar without paying for flight fares or booking hotel accommodations. These types of online seminars are commonly called Webinars.

These days, employees need not be restricted to an office to work. Today's technology allows employees to work from anywhere in the world as though the person is in a physical office. Office spaces are now being eliminated to reduce overhead costs and to improve productivity. These are some of the changes in the information technology.

Constant Changes

On the engineering field, much has also changed. Engineering is constantly being stretched to its limit with the construction of the longest suspension bridge, the tallest building in the world, and the underground transport systems that were not previously imagined as possible. Journey times are tremendously reduced because of efficient transportation systems in place. With the congestion of the ground surface infrastructure, engineers have turned to the underground to develop subsurface infrastructures that have become very vital in the delivery of efficient public service.

While the world appreciates the discoveries of fuel technology such as production of electricity from fossil fuel, the world has moved to conservation of fossil fuel in the name of sustainability. The focus now is on renewable fuel such as solar energy, wind energy, and hydro energy.

A Culture of Positive Change

These sources of energy do not diminish and are in abundance. These are only a few of the changes over the past few decades.

Scientists now understand this universe much better than any other time in history. With the building of each more powerful telescope, more is being learned about the universe. The issue of global warming and its devastating consequences has become an underlining factor for most governmental decisions on development. Global warming and environmental pollution were not great issues in the past few decades. The focus in the past generations was to burn as much coal as possible to generate equivalent electric power possible. Today, that view is changed as the governments of the world are now looking at clean sources of energy.

Yes, these changes have taken place over the decades. With each change come challenges. Just in case you happen to be among those who think or believe that all discoveries have been done, then get ready as I reveal some eye-opening areas of discovery and opportunities.

Every discovery is as a response to a challenge. Therefore, hidden in each challenge is an opportunity. If you work consistently on the opportunity long enough without quitting, the world would soon celebrate you. Every problem opens a door of opportunity. Have you been disappointed over your Internet service? Has your journey been cancelled because of snow fall? Do you think you are paying too much for utilities? If your answer to these questions is yes, then you are staring at opportunities you can work on and change.

The world has yet to discover what could make transportation by flight, rail, and road journeys not affected by snow fall. You can be the person to bring it to limelight. The transportation system is still much dependent on gasoline and diesel as fuel. Electric and hydrogen vehicles are also being manufactured. I believe that a time will come when men and women will not need vehicles to travel but will travel in special suits at a certain height above the ground. The problem would be mid-air collisions, but that can be regulated and controlled.

It is normal for vehicles to have air bags that pop out on impact. These air bags are presently installed in cars to protect occupants. However, accidents still happen and vehicles get compressed and eventually destroy the air bags. I see an opportunity to also create air bags on the outside of vehicles to protect the vehicles and occupants by diffusing the impact upon collision. These air bags will be sensor-sensitive and would pop out as the car approaches a collision point with another object. This discovery will save the car from major damage and also protect the occupants from injury. This is an opportunity waiting to be harnessed.

A quick chemistry lesson: in the school of chemistry, there are some chemical reactions that release heat into the atmosphere. These reactions are said to be exothermic. Also, there are some reactions that absorb heat from the atmosphere. These are said to be endothermic. Exothermic reaction produces heat just like summer weather releases heat into the atmosphere. Endothermic reaction absorbs heat just like winter absorbs heat energy from the atmosphere. The heat produced during summer has been effectively utilized by engineers and builders to heat up houses and save energy through a principle called thermal mass. However, the winter cold remains an unwanted problem. Winter cold is negative energy, so much positive energy is required to warm up houses. I see a very good opportunity to discover an effective use of the winter negative energy. You could be the one to discover a sustainable way to convert the negative energy into a positive energy. Once that is done, people will embrace winter the way summer is embraced. The person who discovers a use for the winter cold has solved a world problem and would be immortalized.

Many opportunities exist in the use of renewable energy. I believe renewable energy can be amplified so that a small amount of energy, such as solar energy, can be amplified by about one thousand times the original value. It is an opportunity waiting to be tapped. I also see another big opportunity in the renewable industry. It is a known fact that sunlight in the temperate regions is not as intense as in the tropics. I see an opportunity where some form of wireless device will tap the abundant solar energy from the tropical zone and channel it to a renewable energy storage facility in the temperate region. In the oil and gas industries, the directional drilling principle is being used to drill oil from a reservoir using a well head located in another country. This principle can be applied to the renewable energy industry by directionally harvesting the abundant solar energy from the tropical continents to the temperate continents. As the world develops, so also the challenges and the opportunities increase.

7

There Is No Luxury of Time

I read on the Internet about a guy advertising that he "had luxury of time, but no teacher." He was going through a period of unemployment, so he decided to use the time he had at his disposal to perfect his playing of the violin. He noticed that he wasn't getting much done by just playing the violin over and over without a teacher, so he went on the Internet seeking helpful tips.

On the other hand, some people do not have enough time to accomplish all their activities. They resort to getting external help to do such things as laundry, dog walking, grocery shopping, babysitting, meal delivery, etc. To these, there is never enough time.

During an academic season, if you ask a college or university student how much time he or she needs to do all that needs to be done, the story will be that the twenty-four hours in a day is not enough to get all things done. During school holidays, if you ask the same student the same question, the answer will be that he or she is bored—there is so much time doing nothing at home.

These scenarios show what time means to different people and how different people use time. No matter how much time is available or unavailable, there are some basic facts about time that I would like to bring to your attention. Understanding these facts will help you manage your time better.

Time Management

The first fact is that available time is constant. There are twenty-four hours in each day and that does not change. This fact only leaves us one option; to plan our program within the time available to us each day. We cannot therefore pretend to be choked by time if we do proper planning and time management. We do not need any more than the time already available to succeed in life. The twenty-four hours we have every day is adequate to live a successful life, if well utilized.

There are three ways to look at time: investing time, spending time, or wasting time. For whatever activity you are involved in, your time is used in one of these three ways. The interpretation or application of the three ways may mean different things to different people.

To explain the ways further, I would say that when you are studying or working in a paid employment or in a voluntary job, the time you use doing those activities is invested. You may either be investing your time or spending your time when you are watching a football game or soccer match, depending on what value you derive from it. You may be either spending or wasting your time when you use hours drinking at a pub or in a night club.

While each of the ways time is used has its own role in a person's life, the most rewarding is when time is invested. It is scary to think that the value any person will exchange for any day of his or her life is spending the day in prison or detention. The time one uses in serving a prison term is wasted if there is no reformation in the person. It may be seen as time invested if the person becomes reformed for the better after the prison term.

The second fact about time is that with each twenty-four-hour day that passes, we exchange a day of our life for it. That day can never be revisited as it goes into the past forever. The way we apply our time each day determines what our tomorrow shall become. We have no control of our yesterday because it is gone forever. We have control of our today and more importantly, our tomorrow because it has not come. What we do in each day is the value we exchange for one day of our life. If we spend a whole day sleeping or lying in bed, that is the value we exchange for that day of our life. It is important to understand that our activity in each day that passes is the value we pay for that day of our life. The question to ask ourselves: *Did we invest our today, or did we waste our today?*

Another fact about time is that time is in constant motion. While we may take a break to rest or to take a vacation from our job, time does not go on holiday or take a break for a deserved rest. Time is constantly on the move. With each tick of the second, the minute, the hour, the day and the year, time passes into history. Time is outside our control. The passage of time brings the seasons. Humankind cannot change the seasons, but instead has learned to plan around the seasons. It is important to understand that time waits for no one. A day cannot be longer or shorter than twenty-four hours. It is constant and continuous. As previously mentioned, while we may take some time off for a deserved rest, break, or holiday, bear in mind that time never goes on break and does not wait on us or for us.

Race against Time

The moment we draw our first breath here on earth, we start a personal race against time. The first twenty-five years of a person's life are the formation years, which are used in character development and personal training. The next twenty-five years is used to build and develop a family. The remaining years are used to define who the person is and to accomplish a purpose. If humankind was to live for about three hundred years, we could afford to waste about two hundred years messing around—but this is not the case.

A human's average life expectancy is about seventy to eighty years. From the moment someone is born and grows up to acquire basic education and training, raising and developing a family, and finally settling down to face life as we know it, the person is already fifty years of age and there is little time to accomplish dreams. There is a race against time. I am aware that some people exceed the one hundred year mark, and I admire that. I have heard some people say that they would not like to live beyond eighty years as they feel they would be too fragile and unfit for life at that age. My view is different. I hope to live for one hundred and twenty years and still be strong and fit at that age.

Time is of the essence in accomplishing success. It is better to be honored while alive rather than to receive an award posthumously. When a person delays in discovering his or her purpose for living, it is most likely that the person may not complete the project of accomplishing dreams due to lifespan limitations. There are occasions in a person's life when the person wished that he or she had started a project twenty years earlier. This often happens when someone catches a vision much later in life. The vision may be something like a philanthropic foundation that would improve other people's lives and provide fulfillment to the visionary. However, because the visionary started the project at the age of fifty or much later, it became obvious that the person will not complete the project because of the race against time. Time is of the essence if we are to accomplish any meaningful success here on earth.

Most successful people I have studied commenced their pursuit of success at an early age; people like J.D. Rockefeller, Warren Buffett, Bill Gates, Thomas Edison, and Richard Branson. Most musical superstars start their careers at a very tender age as well. Even athletes start at a young age to pursue their careers. It is important to begin early to give adequate consideration to what you would like to achieve or become. It is very easy for a person to realize much later in life that time has been stolen—as time waits for no one. Many people suddenly realize that they are too old to complete a project they started.

Do not wait until you are thirty years of age before you begin to seriously consider achieving a meaningful and fulfilling life. The world is waiting and expecting your contribution toward making the earth a better place. The earlier, the better.

There are twenty-four hours in a day. Eight hours are used for sleeping, another eight hours for work, while the last set of eight hours is used at each person's discretion. The difference in the status of each person depends on what each person does with the eight hours at his or her discretion. A man who has lived for ninety years has slept for thirty years of his life. If he worked until retirement, then he had also worked thirty years of his life. In a man's ninety years of life, he had about thirty years to spend time with his family, enjoy leisure, and fulfill his purpose. There is no time to accommodate waste. And for those who spend about one hour every day to travel to work, the available time to their discretion is even smaller. There is no luxury of time.

Life is about Balance

Imagine someone who has worked hard all his life until he is now a top management staff in an oil exploration company. He tells his family that his employer provides the family's provision, so he has to put his work as top priority. He boasts to his friends that he is a top management staff in a big corporation because he has put everything into his career.

This attitude started back when he was in secondary school. He always had his notebooks with him and read them at every opportunity. He did not join others when it was time for games or recreation; he would go to some quiet place to read. No wonder he was at the top of his class and gained immediate admission into the university. The same attitude continued at the university, which made him graduate with honors. After university, he received an offer to join a multinational oil exploration company. In all his youth, he never got involved in social activities. His wife was the first woman who got close to him—thanks to his cousin, who introduced them.

Now, as a top level manager, his workaholic attitude is taking a toll on his family, his wife, two sons, and a daughter. He comes home many evenings with more work to do, and has no time to play or talk with his family. People around and in the office call him "Mr. Serious," because he always looks serious and is in a pensive mood. His children seem far from him and very close to their mother. When 'Mr. Serious' is not sleeping, he is working. Even his discussions with his wife are all about his work. He says things such as, "My Corporation is bringing in another drilling rig, and I have to be spot-on during the installation. I hope to send my team on further training in order to get it right." Normally, his wife would not respond. Or she may say, "Junior performed very well in his exams; I think we should take him out for some fun." The man would reply, "He has to be like his father. That was how I performed in school to be in this position that I am today," then he would go off to his home office and work the rest of the evening.

The last time he took his family on a holiday was when he had a two week official training abroad. He took his family so that while he was in training, his wife could wander around the city with the kids.

A Culture of Positive Change

From this story, you may get a feeling that something is not right despite the man's success in his career. His life is out of balance. His childhood foundation was not adequate, which has also affected his adulthood.

Imagine another person who was pampered to go through primary school. He progressed to secondary school but had to drop out in the second year. He preferred to learn some trade rather than go to school. After dropping out of school, he spent the following three years at home, spending most of his time playing games and sleeping. His mother home-taught him, but each session did not last more than thirty minutes, as he preferred to play games instead. Now he is in his early twenties and working in a pub. He is still living with his mother who provides all the feeding and house expenses for him. His room has a 32-inch flat screen television connected to his computer for games. He works in the pub for a four-hour shift and spends the rest of the day on his game table. He is currently having problems with his childhood girlfriend. She complains that he does not do enough to make a living and be a man. The guy thinks that the only reason he needs to work is to get money for hanging out with friends, since his mother provides all that he needs. His girlfriend does not see a future with him.

From the narrative of these two men, we can deduce that there were some forms of imbalance in their lifestyles. One was the extreme of "all work and no play," and the other was the extreme of "all play and no work." Between these two extremes lies a perfect balance for a life of success and fulfillment. As mentioned previously, there are twenty-four hours in a day (including night). If separated into three, there are three parts of eight hours each. It is well advised that eight hours sleep is good for healthy existence. It is also mostly agreed that an eight-hour work day is best and most businesses adhere to that timing. That leaves the last eight hours in every day at the discretion of each individual.

The difference in the life of each individual and the status of every person in life is determined primarily by what each individual does with the remaining eight hours. Put in another way, for emphasis, the success or failure of each individual hinges primarily on what each person does with the eight free hours at his or her discretion. In the two stories cited, one man used the remaining eight hours for work, while the other used his for play. That was the reason both of those individuals had problems in their lives. To achieve success in life, you must be able to utilize your eight hours in a balanced way to add value to your life, your family, and your neighbourhood.

Some people argue that in a day, eight hours is for sleep, eight hours is for work, and the remaining eight hours is for play. That is fine if you just want to be ordinary. But if you want your life to be counted among the legends, those who achieved beyond the ordinary, those who refused to be dictated by the economic policies of the government, then you may need to reconsider how best to use the eight hours of your day. It makes all the difference!

You require those eight hours to create balance and harmony in your life. You need those eight hours to study, to know more than your competitors. You need those eight hours to spend time with and show love to your family. You need those eight hours to maintain good relationships with friends. Most importantly, you need those eight hours at your discretion to discover who you are and to express who you are. The way you utilize those eight hours is completely decided by you—and they determine who and what you become.

8

You Have to Make the Hard Decisions

I used to regularly go to the gym and work out. I had friends who also worked out and sometimes we would relax and chill out after our gym session and chat about general issues. Roberto had some unwanted weight he was trying to shed, while Tony was actually a bit on the thin side. If going to the gym was just for losing weight, then Tony had no need for the gym. However, Tony seemed to be more frequent than the rest of us.

One day we were having coffee in the leisure center when Roberto said he'd rather not come to the gym but he wanted to get into better shape and fitness.

"Nothing comes easy," Tony told Roberto.

"If I looked like you, nobody would see me at this gym," Roberto told Tony.

"It's taken me a long time to get this thin and in shape. I've been coming to the gym a long time to remain this way," Tony replied.

"You must have really been dedicated to maintaining your physique," I said to Tony.

"To accomplish anything in life requires some form of dedication," Tony added, addressing no one in particular.

"When I close my eyes, I see myself the way I want to look—the finished picture. That is the drive that keeps me coming to the gym regularly," said Roberto.

"I feel good with my body after every work-out; that is my motivation," I added.

"For me, I just want to stay fit; that drives me to the gym regularly," Tony told us.

If you follow the discussion that I had with my gym friends, you quickly realize that each of us had made a decision to work out in the gym. The decision was not pleasant, but because of what we intend to achieve, we are dedicated to stick to that decision. Success in life never comes on a platter of gold. If you ask those who were born with silver or golden spoons in their mouths, they would tell you that it is difficult to maintain inherited wealth. If you are not trained in the ways of managing success, inherited wealth may add more problems than it solves.

If you wish to climb to the pinnacle of success and achievement, you must be able to make the hard decisions.

I have called them *hard* because some may see them as deprivations from fun; but in reality, fun sometimes stands in the way of success if not checked.

What are these hard decisions?

When I was an undergraduate, one of my lecturers gave my class advice that he said was also given to him by his lecturer when he was an undergraduate. Mine was an engineering class and it happened that we had no girls in class. He advised us to make the decision to focus on our studies and do without chasing after girls, binge drinking, cult activities, and other social vices. These things, he said, would cause us to derail from succeeding in our studies. He said if we focused on our studies and eventually succeed in life, girls and other good things would line up seeking our attention. The same also applies to young women. I felt pleased with the fact that girls would be seeking after me if I became successful. At that time we were struggling to get girlfriends. To know that girls would be at my disposal if I achieved success was gratifying.

I have grown up to know that the advice from my undergraduate lecturer was true and relevant to anyone who wishes to achieve success. One of the attractions of success is relationships with the opposite sex. Success has a way of rewarding those who achieve it with good measures of those things they forfeited in the attainment of success. Every superstar has difficulties managing admirers.

This is not the case with those who get distracted and do not succeed. Nobody wants to put up with failure. The fruit that failure produces is deprivation. It's difficult for people to hang around failure for long. That is why you don't want to be tagged a failure—rather do what is necessary—make the hard decisions now so you will be rewarded later.

You've got to make the hard decision in order to succeed. The decision is to stop anything on your path to success before it stops you. It is better to deprive yourself some fun as a youth and to enjoy the rest of your life, than to enjoy some fun as a youth and suffer deprivation for the rest of your life.

The hard decisions are not just about choosing the kind of friends you have. They also include choosing not to get into cults, gangs, or other social vices. They are decisions about how much time you give to the social media, TV, and games. You must make a lifestyle change that will focus your energy on your dream. Hard decisions are all about balancing your life with a positive tilt toward achieving your dreams.

A colleague of mine has a passion for playing soccer. He rarely trades his training for anything else. To achieve success in any endeavor, you have to refuse distractions. You have to maintain your focus on the goal and the crown.

Rediscover Your Childhood Dreams

If you ask any child what he or she hopes to be as an adult, the child will readily give you an answer such as, "I want to be a famous basketball player," or "I would like to be an airplane pilot." There are no lack of answers that children give regarding their choice of dream careers, which may be influenced from someone or something in the child's life. For instance, a child may wish to be a carpenter because someone came and fixed their broken kitchen door. A child may choose to be a pilot because the parents took the child on holiday in an airplane. Another child may choose to be a doctor because the child heard doctors make a lot of money. A little kid may tell you today, "I want to be a teacher when I grow up," and the next day may say, "I want to be a musician when I grow up." They are children; there is no long-term thought process involved when they say what they want to become when they grow up. However, this is the beginning of our childhood dreams.

When children start attending school, they become exposed to career guidance and parental advice. At this stage children begin to put some thought into a choice of career. Those who are technically inclined may begin to consider becoming engineers. The ones with interest in stage performance or music may choose a career in the respective fields of interest. Some children will learn a trade of their choice. The career choices that young people make after career guidance and parental direction are toward achieving a certain target, a *dream*. This dream is what decides the course to study in the university or a trade to learn.

As a young child I had the dream of becoming a children's doctor—a pediatrician. I believe I formed this opinion when my parents took me to a doctor because I was not feeling well, and he made me feel better. I decided that I was going to be a doctor and even made it known to my parents and brothers. When I was preparing to be admitted into a university, I put medicine as my first choice of course. Due to the competitive nature of the course, I did not gain admission in my first attempt. Something happened, however, that made me change my course to engineering. Today I am an engineer, and I look back and thank God for the events that made me change from medicine to engineering. I believe I am more fulfilled being an engineer than I would have been as a doctor.

The point I am trying to drive home is that most children have a childhood dream—not a dream that takes place when asleep. This dream is a mental picture of who we desire to become. It is the end product of a personality. The good thing about childhood dreams is that a child does not consider the process of achieving the dream. It's more of setting the end from the beginning. This is the easy part—and also the necessary part in achieving the dream.

The road toward achieving any dream is lined with challenges. Many people give up on their dreams while traveling along this road. Others get distracted and turn away from their destination and take route to some other destination. What many people do not understand is that the challenges are part of the grand design toward achieving a dream. A salesman may need ten 'no' answers before a getting a 'yes' answer. With each 'no' he receives, he learns how to do it better. When he finally gets a 'yes' at the eleventh presentation, his life is changed forever as he progresses to achieve his dream of being salesman of the year. Imagine if he had given up at the ninth or tenth 'no' he received; his dream would have been aborted. This is what happens to many people.

Many give up on their dream when they are so close to success. Some people have told me that they plan to drop out of school because it is too difficult. When I ask about their next plan, most respond that they have no plan apart from dropping out of school.

I was traveling in an overcrowded bus recently and was standing beside two men who were sharing some deep personal thoughts. I heard one say that his childhood dream was to be a musician. That was all he wanted to do. He started playing in pubs and gigs but soon decided that he needed to also get a job. He got a job as a bartender and was combining his musical performance with bar service. Soon he had less time performing as he spent more and more hours working in the bar. He told his friend that he was full of regret for not pursuing his childhood dream. He said he still remembered the joy he had after each performance and the wild crowds that attended his shows. His friend told him that bar service still gets him to meet different people. "No! It's not the same thing," he jumped in before his friend concluded the sentence. "It has to do with fulfillment. I now realize that I was more fulfilled doing shows than serving in the bar," he concluded. "I wonder if I can still play the guitar anymore," he said.

As I quietly listened to these two friends share their thoughts, I wondered how many people, like the one guy, have lost their childhood dreams and now regret it. If you are a teenager, you can probably confirm that there is a certain personality you are aspiring to become as an adult. It is that personality I call a childhood dream.

A Culture of Positive Change

If it is true that every person had a childhood dream, it means that those who end up in the rehab centers are those who have lost their childhood dreams. Those who are dependent on society rather than contributing to the society probably lost their childhood dreams.

To accomplish a childhood dream requires focus and the determination to make the hard decisions. There will be some distraction along the road, but focus keeps you on track. There will be challenges and difficulties on the way, but determination will keep you going. As you follow after a dream, situations will arise that may make you refine the dream. It is ok to refine or redefine a dream based on improved knowledge or change in circumstances. What is not ok is when you have no dream or pursuit in life. Life becomes an empty chase of "what will be will be." No matter what the circumstance is, do not live without a dream for the future. Your childhood dream may change with time, but make sure you have a dream.

Don't Grow Old, Grow Up

One important day in every person's life is the birth day. The birthday anniversary is the celebration of the addition of one year to the celebrant's life. Children look forward to their birthday celebration as a day of fun and receiving gifts from parents and friends. It is a day of joy for every child. Some people with the resources celebrate their birthdays annually with lavish entertainment for guests and well-wishers. Whether it is 1st birthday or 100th birthday, the story is the same. It is a celebration for how long the individual has lived here on earth.

A birthday celebration marks advancement in age. It simply says that a person is getting older. Nature has linked age advancement to physical and psychological development. As children get older, they learn to walk and talk, then they reach school age. School curriculum is designed to correspond to the age of the children. As they get older, they are expected to know and understand certain subjects, under normal circumstances.

Certain behaviors are expected from people at different ages in life. For instance, there is a certain age when a person is expected to move from being dependent on parents to being independent. There is a certain age when a person is expected to contribute positively in the society. A time comes when people are expected to have their own family and be responsible parents. Responsibility ought to come with advancement in age.

Responsibility ought to come with advancement in age.

Sadly enough, it's not every person who grows up. Some people simply just grow old. Imagine someone who just turned thirty-nine years and still lives in his parents' house. The person does not have any disability or medical condition. He simply did not like the "stress" from school, so he dropped out. He refused to learn a trade because it was so much "hassle." The parents had kept a close eye on him to prevent him from going into dangerous drinking. This was the reason the parents have also maintained him in their house. The years just roll by with no plans of things getting better. The guy is simply growing old and not growing up.

A Culture of Positive Change

This case is a too-common scenario, portraying what is happening in our societies today. Street corners are filled with people who have stopped growing up—and are only growing old. To these people, there is no improvement to their situation or plans for improvement. Some of these people are constantly under influence of drugs or alcohol that keeps their minds from functioning correctly.

The moment the mind stops functioning correctly, the person stops growing up. That is what happens when someone who used to be a pop star or a respected actor or actress becomes a drug addict. You may have heard stories of people who were idols to the younger generation suddenly are in drug rehabilitation centers. People under the influence of drugs or alcohol have lost the rational control of their minds. Such people only grow old—they do not grow up. There is no progress without a sound mind.

It is not only drugs and alcohol that cause someone to stop growing up. Drugs and alcohol problems usually start at a later stage in a person's life; mostly after the person becomes independent from parental control. However, for a child still with the parents, there are several things that the child could do that would make him or her only grow old and not grow up correspondingly. When a child refuses to go to school, the child is simply growing old and not growing up. When a child joins a local gang or terror group, the child has chosen not to grow up but to grow old only. Sooner than later, the child may end up in a detention center. A child who ran away from home to live on the streets has chosen to stop growing up—and will only grow old.

It is a natural process to grow up physically and psychologically with each passing year. However, growth in terms of personal development requires some effort and commitment, and depends on individual aspirations. For instance, everybody forty years old does not have the same level of success. That means that the levels to which people grow is dependent on each person's motivation, focus, and determination—not on their physical age.

Life is a Journey to a Destination

Consider a ship docked in a harbor and about to set sail to a far destination. The voyage has been mapped out in detail. The captain of the ship and the crew know exactly how long the journey will take. They know that there will be waves and turbulence on the journey, but they also understand that the ship has been built to withstand the turbulence. The captain of the ship knows in detail the exact route to navigate the ship in order to arrive at the destination. Some routes may present greater sea turbulence than others. The captain knows the routes with less turbulence and will navigate through such routes. The captain and the crew have brought along enough sustenance for the duration of the journey. They have everything planned and organized.

They achieved the goal they set out to accomplish. The ship arrived at its destination and delivered the cargo.

Imagine another ship about to set out on a similar journey. This time there is no captain, no crew members, and no set destination. No proper plan was made for the ship to get to a specific destination. The ship was just allowed to start sailing. There is no doubt that this ship will be tossed to and fro by the waves. The ship may make some motion, but without forward progress. Its movement will be decided by the direction of the tidal flow. The ship may get into heavy turbulence and may be shipwrecked or may get stuck on some sandy beach. It will never get to a destination. It will never deliver the cargo.

The ships I have described are like the human life. Every person is the captain of his or her life. Every person is navigating his or her life to a certain destination. The destination is different for each person. Each person determines the destination. Each person's destination is what the person hopes to become in life.

The cargo is the achievements or accomplishments we deliver as we sail toward our destination. Our cargo includes the lives we touch in positive ways. The cargo is the potential we possess to improve others' lives. Everybody carries cargo. Everybody has the potential to deliver the cargo to a desired destination. However, not everybody makes it to a desired destination. Not everybody delivers the cargo they bear.

Everybody at some early stage in life have some novelty idea of what to become or achieve in life. As a child, there is ambition bubbling inside about how great we hope to become. Every child is guilty of this regardless of background or family history. Those who achieve their childhood dreams took control of their lives. They followed their dreams with plans and actions to achieve their dreams. When they encountered challenges on their way, they did not give up. They understood that they were already equipped to overcome the challenges. So when the challenges of financial hardship came, they pressed on. When the challenges of peer pressure came, they kept to their goals. When the challenges of bullying came, they did not give up. When the challenges of a broken home came, they were not deterred. They were determined to get to their destination and to deliver their cargo. These are the ones who became the great inventors, doctors, engineers, philanthropists, and athletes. These are the ones who made medical discoveries. They excelled in whatever profession they chose for themselves. They reached their destination by adequate planning and being in control of their lives every step of the way.

You can be one of those! Maybe your community needs a soup kitchen to provide meals for disadvantaged people or a used clothing outlet for families in distress; maybe your school needs teacher assistants to spend time with students with learning disabilities; maybe your church needs painted or the plumbing fixed. You can make a difference in the lives of others in many different ways.

I mentioned earlier that every child is guilty of having a childhood fantasy of who he or she wishes to become. Consequently, every adult once had a childhood dream. Many adults never realize their childhood dreams. They never delivered their cargo. The potential they possessed was never realized. Some of these adults end up sitting on the street corners depending on the charity of others. Some are locked up in prisons serving prison terms for crimes committed. Some are hooked on hard drugs and barely exist without these drugs. Like the ship I described that set sail without a captain and was tossed to and fro by every wind and sea wave, these people have lost control of their lives. Their lives are decided by whatever circumstance they find themselves in at any point in time.

They lost control when they did not make the hard decisions and make a plan to get to their destination or to achieve their dreams. Without a plan and a goal to achieve the plan, it becomes difficult to withstand challenges along the way. When the challenge of bullying at school came, they gave up and dropped out of school to the care of "mommy," and gave in to self-pity. I am not saying that bullying should be tolerated, but anyone being bullied should see it as a challenge and fight to conquer it. Do not let bullying rob you of your desire to accomplish great things.

Deliver Your Cargo

Many who lost control of their lives succumbed to peer pressure of indulgence into irresponsible behavior. They knew they were steering away from their dream but chose not to correct their course. They never got to their destination, and they never delivered their cargo. They were once children with great ambition and physical well-being but become dependent on others because they lost control of their lives as the journey progressed. Rather than contributing to the society, society contributes to them. Life became a matter of existing rather than living. Sadly, there are millions of these lost ones around the globe—in every country, every culture—ones who will never fulfill their destinies.

> ***Without a set destination, anywhere becomes a destination.***

I had mentioned earlier that all people have the potential to make a contribution in life. That contribution is the cargo that we possess to deliver to our destination. Only those who remain focused toward arriving at their destination will eventually deliver the cargo. Many of those who lost focus and gave up in life will not deliver the cargo they possess. Imagine that the person who could have discovered the vaccine for HIV dropping out from school because he or she was being bullied. That may be the reason for the delay in discovering the vaccine these past decades. Imagine the person who could have discovered an eye operation that would enable blind people to see gave in to peer pressure and drugs, committed crimes, and was sentenced to life in prison. Most crimes are committed by those who have lost control of their destination in life. They took the wrong way rather than making the hard decisions and wandered into the wrong side of life.

It is important for each of us to decide, from a youthful age, our destination in life and to work through the challenges to get to the destination. Without a set destination, anywhere becomes a destination. A destination set by circumstance is almost always not the best. If you want to live life and not just exist, then take control of your destination in life—today.

9

Hints on Discovering Who You Are

No two people are exactly the same. There is no other person in the world who has your exact fingerprints or exact same voice or DNA. You are the original of yourself and there is no copy. It is common to hear youths say they wish they could be like their idol or someone they admire. They say, "I wish I could dance like him," or "I wish I could sing like her." It's good to admire someone and even wish to be like the person—if that person is upright and a good role model. It's good to follow in the footsteps of a person who mentors you or a person who has the values you respect. The truth is, you can never be someone else. The best you would be is an imitator—not a copy. A copy means the exact resemblance of the original. That does not happen with the intrinsic nature of human beings.

Elvis Presley has millions of followers who consider him their idol. Some had wished they were exactly like him. That is not possible because Elvis is the only original. Others who wish to be like him can only imitate him or impersonate him. Michael Jackson had many followers who did everything possible to be like him. There are many Michael Jackson imitators and impersonators, but there is only one original Michael Jackson. The point is that there is only one original of anybody. You are the only original of you—there is no copy.

Many people today do not know who they are. A lot of people spend time and energy trying to be someone they are not instead of focusing on discovering who they are. Some think they have the wrong skin color. Others think they are the wrong sex. Some do not like their hair, their height, their eye color. They simply wish they looked like or were someone else.

Instead of worrying about the things you do not like about yourself or focusing so much energy on how to be like someone you are not, have you tried discovering how you could use your unique features to your advantage? Instead of feeling dejected because you are not tall enough, have you tried to find out the advantages you have because of your height? Everything about you is perfect for your design. If you think you are not tall enough, consider that you are the perfect height for your design. If you were born a boy or a girl, that is because of who you were born to become. If you were born in a neighbourhood with gangs, there may be a purpose for it. You may be the person designed to change your neighbourhood. Do not blame yourself for being born into the neighbourhood, rather discover the purpose why you are there. The reason or purpose for a couple who has a disabled child may be for the couple to develop love and care for the needy. To discover your purpose is to discover who you are.

To discover your purpose is to discover who you are.

It is important to realize that every person is unique with a unique assignment or purpose. The journey to a meaningful life begins with the discovery of self. You've got to discover the person you are to be able to perform what you are designed to accomplish. From the day you discover who you are, you begin to live and not just exist. Discovery of self makes others want to imitate you. You become a pacesetter and an idol to others. There are many people who exist without knowing who they really are. They go into the wrong profession, move to a wrong location, or marry the wrong person. For most of these people, they live to please others rather than fulfilling their destiny. These people wish that life was different and say if they were to have a second chance in life, they would live it differently; but in reality, they are not willing to make the hard decisions and then take steps to change.

When you know who you are and are on the road to reach your destination, you won't want to change a thing if you were given a second chance at living it all over again. Working in the understanding of who you are ushers fulfillment into your life.

When you discover who you are, you begin to live and not just exist.

I understand that it may not seem easy to discover self. However, certain things in each person's life are pointers to discovering self. Discovery of self is a personal journey. Someone else cannot discover who you are. It is personal. I discover who I am and you discover who you are. The process does not call for a desperate search for answers to the numerous questions such as, "Who am I" or "Why am I here?" Discovery of who you are is a process that opens up to you gradually with increasing clarity. I have highlighted some pointers that will help you discover who you are.

A person's inherent talent or natural abilities are indicators of who that person is designed to become. Every person has unique abilities that were deposited as part of the person's genetic make-up. These abilities are not acquired through education but may be developed or enhanced through use and regular practice. There is no person without a unique ability. I know that a lot of people will arguably disagree with me on that statement, but this is because many people do not know what their unique ability is and they struggle to find it.

The challenge is in finding what your unique ability is because everyone surely has at least one. Some of these unique abilities are easily expressible such as athletic skills, good musical voice, unique dance styles, sculpture or artistic skills, teaching abilities, etc. It is very easy to observe these skills in people. However, not everybody has these types of unique abilities that are easily manifested and expressed. There are the unique abilities that may be easily overlooked by those who have them, yet these unique characteristics define them.

Some have smiles that brighten a sad atmosphere. Some have a contagious sense of humor that makes others laugh. There are people who have the gift of kind words; they can talk to someone who is depressed or suicidal and inject a spark of life. There are others who have the patience for listening. Many people do not consider listening a unique ability, but it is a skill that requires patience, which is a virtue. Many people do not have such patience. There are others who have a kind heart for the suffering and poor folks. Others have the ability to provide support and courage to others. Some athletes or musicians may not be successful without the support and courage of some special people in their life. The ability to provide encouragement to someone with a unique talent is on its own, a unique talent. Some have oratory or mediator skills; it takes a special talent to make peace between two nations at war with each other, to talk a hostage taker out of a disastrous end, or make a teenager to understand that his actions will be devastating and life-changing.

I have mentioned these unique abilities so those who think they do not have any talent can re-assess themselves once again and appreciate what they already possess. It is important to mention here that some of these unique abilities may not manifest themselves until it meets an opportunity. For instance, people with a unique care and love for suffering children may not know this about themselves until they come face to face with those suffering children. Such an opportunity will activate the passion that will cause a positive reaction.

Another pointer to discovering who you are, are your dislikes. The things you naturally dislike are indications of who you are or who you ought to be. You may have discovered that some people get angry hearing about an oppressive government. Some get passionately angry over child labor or child abuse. Some people hate to see suffering humanity. These are all indicators of who they are or what their purpose may be. The things we get passionate about may be a call to action. That is why someone like Nelson Mandela risked his life in the fight against apartheid. Missionaries have traveled far and wide risking their lives to help broken humanity because they don't want to see people suffer in ignorance.

In trying to define who you are, think about the things that get you upset each time you see them or think about them. That may be a call to action to try and change things. Nelson Mandela hated to see his Black brothers and sisters being oppressed by the minority White in the South Africa. To him, it was a call to action. That call defined who he is today. Stopping the oppression of his fellow country men and women became a purpose and an assignment for his life.

Martin Luther King Jr. was a pastor who did not like to see his fellow Black brothers and sisters treated as inferior or third class citizens. He believed that all people were born equal. He led a peaceful revolt that shook the foundations of the United States of America to stop the marginalization of Black Americans. Martin Luther King Jr. devoted his life to the struggle for equal right even though he knew that it might cost him his life—which it did. Moses, in the Bible, was raised in Pharaoh's palace in Egypt. However, he hated the oppression of the Israelites by the Egyptians. He became defensive for the Israelites and killed an Egyptian in the process. He later became the leader God used to deliver the Israelites from Egyptian bondage. What you detest passionately is a pointer to your assignment in life.

A Culture of Positive Change

Another pointer toward discovering who you are is the geographical location of your birth and where you were raised. Imagine that you were born in a community where women are marginalized or where it is the custom that women should not be educated. Imagine that you were born in a community where women have no contribution in the choice of their marriage partners or where families give out their female children in marriage without the child's consent. Being born into such an environment does not require that you relocate to a city where women have equal rights to the men. I believe the reason people are born in some locations is because there is a contribution that is required of those people. Discover the contribution you can make in your community—and you may have discovered your purpose, who you are.

Another pointer to a person's assignment in life is the things that the person loves to do. I have a friend who has two sons. One likes to solve puzzles and to build robots, while the other son likes outdoor activities such as football, soccer, and golfing. Anything that we love to talk about or are excited to do may be pointing to our life assignment.

No one is consulted prior to birth about being a male or female. No one is consulted prior to birth about the choice of parents or a geographical location preference. No one has any input on the shape of his or her face or their height as an adult. Everyone grows to discover their parents, place of birth, facial features, and other physical characteristics such as height and color of skin. Some people grow to hate who they become. For this reason, there is an increase of those who want to go under the surgeon's knife for such things as a sex change and physical enhancements. Instead of spending resources and energy being angry with the image you see in the mirror or asking questions why you were born to such horrible parents, it is more beneficial to channel that energy and resources toward discovering the purpose of who you are.

I had the opportunity to listen to a young man in his early twenties who was worried that he had some form of anti-social behavior. This young university undergraduate said that he believed strongly that he had a social problem because he could not freely join his friends in binge drinking or doing some other activities that his friends did when they were drunk. I asked him to explain what he meant to help me understand why he was getting depressed. The young man told me that he got along better with older people than he did with his same-age friends. He preferred mature music rather than music enjoyed by people his age. He told me that he could not drink to get drunk. This aspect of not being able to binge drink worried him because while his friends were drinking and chatting, he was on his own since he would stop drinking much sooner than his friends.

He mentioned that he felt alone when he attended parties with his friends because almost everyone would get drunk or tipsy as the party progressed. With time his friends and other people in the party would head in different directions, in pairs, while he was alone. This frustrated him as he seemed to be the only one not having fun. For these reasons, the student felt as if he had a social problem and was getting depressed. When I asked him if he had given thought to not joining his friends at parties or drinking outing, he said that would make things worse for him—he would feel even more isolated.

I won't bother telling you how the young man was made to understand who he was and that he was unique as he was, but he did and was relieved of depression. Many people are in the same situation as this young man. They want to "belong" by living a lie. They live lives not meant for them. In trying to belong to some social, cultural, religious, or elite groups, many people fail to realize who they were made to be. A set of identical twins may have completely opposite temperaments. One of the twins may be introverted and likes being alone, while the other may be extroverted and likes crowds. It would be hard for each twin to live the other's life, even though they are identical twins.

Life is more fulfilling when each person understands what makes him or her unique and original. A person who likes quietness needs it to become who he or she was made to be. An outgoing person needs it to become who he or she was made to be. To understand who you are, you need to sit down with yourself and understand the life you like living. If you are being influenced by your friends to live a life you know you don't enjoy, you should be truthful with yourself and discover the life that is meant for you. Do not live like a party-goer if you know you don't enjoy it. Do not live like a workaholic if you know you don't enjoy it. Living a false life only delays or derails you from your destiny. Be real.

Self-Discovery Ideas

I love it when I have some ideas in my head that just won't go away. I mean ideas of things I wish to accomplish that have not yet materialized. I call such ideas, dreams or visions. Some of these dreams are so big that they look practically impossible at the moment. Thinking of these dreams empowers me and helps me to channel my energy and resources appropriately.

Dreams that are so strong inside of you that refuse to vanish are strong indicators toward discovering who you are. Dreams and visions help us accomplish our purpose. The world as it is today has been shaped by men and women who did not let their dreams die. They followed after their dream, thereby fulfilling their purpose. It was a strong dream for the Wright Brothers to get a metal contraption to fly in the air. They followed after their dream and developed the airplane. In following after their dream, they discovered who they were and fulfilled their purpose. Dreams that won't go away are sometimes strong pointer toward self-discovery.

Thomas Edison dreamed of discovering an electric light that everyday people could afford to buy. Henry Ford dreamed of building an automobile assembly operation that would result in affordable vehicles. It was almost impossible for an individual to own a personal computer around 1975. Bill Gates and his partner dreamed of placing a personal computer on every desk and in every household. Today, people worldwide are enjoying the reality of those dreams come true. Those dreams defined who they were and their purpose in life. Following after your dream and accomplishing it will define who you are and the purpose you have to achieve.

I mentioned previously that some persistent dreams look practically impossible or unrealistic. However, no dream is bigger than the dreamer. If you can dream it, you can accomplish it. It is your responsibility to make dreams become real. Do not allow the size of your dream deter you. Every big dream comes in little parts that if put together, will realize the dream.

If you can dream it, you can accomplish it.

It's possible that you have carried the dream of being the best doctor in your country from the time you were in primary school until now when you are in college. The dream will come with ideas about how to make it happen, such as performing well in school. If your dream is to own a company that manufactures quality construction products, then the little parts of this dream may be that you have to work in a construction product manufacturing company to gain experience. It may be that you need to take loan to buy some equipment or start in your garage. Every dream, no matter how big, provides you with the parts or ideas toward realizing the dream. In fulfilling those persistent dreams that you have, you will be discovering who you are and also fulfilling the purpose for your life.

Dare to be Different

One of the greatest enemies of success is conformity. This is because nobody wants to be the "odd person out." People are scared to deviate from the perceived norm; things have to be done in a certain way. Every society is known for its customs and traditions. Therefore operating outside the generally accepted norms of the society will raise eyebrows. The government sets its rules and policies by which its people are governed. It becomes an offense to operate outside the set rules. Every firm has its policies and procedures by which every employee must comply. Operating outside the company policies and procedures attracts disciplinary action.

In some societies, women are not permitted to drive vehicles. Some cultures expect a younger person to stand up from a chair once an elder person walks into the room. In other cultures, it is expected that a younger person bow before an elder person as a sign of respect. Other cultures expect a younger person to join both hands while shaking the hand of an older person. The list of traditions is inexhaustible and varies from society to society. As a result of all these scenarios, the creative and imaginative part of the human mind tends to be dormant or put to rest. People are forced to conform to whatever is the perceived norm. There is reluctance to initiate a change or to be seen as different. People just flow: business as usual.

One of the greatest enemies of success is conformity.

Conforming to the unwritten laws of the society makes us like everybody else; buried in the crowd. Society does not honor conformists, but those who are different. The queen will never honor a conformist but only those who have achieved extraordinary accomplishment by daring to be different. Every success and accomplishment begins when people decide to be different. By daring to be different, I mean that you dare to be yourself and not be like anybody else. Daring to be yourself will surely make you different

A Culture of Positive Change

because every person is unique. A champion is the person who dares to be himself or herself. Achievers set their own standards. They do not just do things because everyone is doing the same thing. It is possible that everyone is wrong and just did not know it. An achiever keeps his or her head when others are losing theirs and blaming it on the achiever. Be not a conformist, be a pacesetter.

Society had long lied to us that some humans are superior and more important than others. For many years this lie ruled in the hearts of men and women until someone who dared to be different stood up against the lie. Today, it is generally believed in most parts of the world that all humanity is created equal. Upon this truth Martin Luther King Jr. refused to accept the oppression of his people as being inferior and second-class humans. He refused to conform to oppression.

The current United States of America, President, Barack Obama, is a person who was different from the time he was born. He was born to an African father and a White mother. Obama was quoted as saying that his father looked nothing like the people around him; being black as pitch while his mother was white as milk. Obama's father lived with his mother for about three years before his parents separated. His mother remarried an Indonesian, where Obama started his early education until he was ten years of age. Obama returned to the United States to live with his maternal grandparents while his mother remained in Indonesia.

His childhood and teenage years present logical arguments for such a child to be a failure. As a young adult, Obama said he struggled to reconcile social perceptions of his multiracial heritage. This resulted in his using drugs and alcohol to push questions of who he was, out of his mind. If Obama had turned out to be a failure, in my opinion, it would have been justifiable considering his background. Many people today relapse into drug use and alcohol because they are born to a single parent or because they have a background such as Obama's. People give up in life or become depressed with the excuse that they were abandoned by their father. Obama's story is not better. What do you expect of a child who was abandoned by his father before he was three years and abandoned by his mother when the child was ten years? The entire scenario presents a boy who would probably become a criminal. But not for this boy who dared to be different.

Obama rose beyond his discouraging background to become president of the Harvard Law Review. He progressed after earning his law degree to representing the 13th district of the State of Illinois. He went on to become a United States senator and finally the president of the United States of America. Barack Obama's story is an encouraging one that tells us that dreams can come true if we dare to stand out and not believe the lies of society. Obama went through the process of self-discovery until he came to the point when he told himself that his background could not hold him back. He saw so much potential in himself that he could not let his pitiable background dictate what or who he became. He dared to be different. He dared to be himself, and that made his uniqueness stand out.

A Culture of Positive Change

If only you dare to be yourself, you will discover that you are different.

The story of Helen Keller is an amazing story of a young American girl who dared to be different despite her disability. Helen was born a normal child but became sick when she was just nineteen months old. The sickness that lasted for a short time left Keller deaf and blind. She became a living mute, as there was no way to communicate with her. Ann Sullivan was recruited to be Helen's teacher. Communication with a deaf-blind mute was almost impossible. Ann taught her to finger-spell by using Keller's finger to spell out words. It was difficult for Keller to understand what the words meant. The breakthrough came when Sullivan poured water over Keller's palm while she finger-spelled the word water on her free hand. This event suddenly revealed to Helen the mystery of language. She became inquisitive and wanted to know the name of almost every object she touched.

Helen Keller continued her progress and enrolled into college. She was the first deaf-blind person to enroll in an institution of higher learning. She was also the first deaf-blind person to earn a Bachelor of Arts degree. Keller became a renowned author and traveled around the world delivering lectures about how she dared to be different. She wrote, "The public must learn that the blind man is neither genius nor a freak nor an idiot. He has a mind that can be educated, a hand which can be trained, and ambitions which it is right for him to strive to realize, and it is the duty of the public to help him make the best of himself so that he can win light through work."

John Iroh

Helen Keller achieved what most people without a disability could not achieve. And she made it difficult for people to use disability as an excuse for not having personal dreams and ambitions—and for not achieving such dreams and ambitions. Keller did not allow the frustration of being locked out from the world to stop her from realizing her personal ambitions. She dared to be different!

10

And Finally

The law of diminishing intent is a popular saying that states: *the longer you delay in taking action on anything you wish to do, the higher the likelihood that you will never take the action*. Think about this statement. Does it seem to apply to you in anyway at all? For instance, have you ever decided to go to the gym at least three times a week to get back the "six-pack" stomach you once had? You were excited at the thought and you planned to start on Monday. Monday came and you thought to yourself that the weather was not good and that you would start on Tuesday. You later decided to let the week pass and that you would definitely commence the next Monday. It's now a month since you had the intent but the enthusiasm is gone because of the delay in taking action.

Or have you planned to move to your own flat and become independent from your parents? Maybe you discussed your plans with your parents and you were very excited at the thought of moving into your own flat. One year after the initial intent you are still living with your parents, and you are not sure anymore when you will have your own flat.

Those are examples of the law of diminishing intent at work. Another instance: Perhaps you smoke twenty cigarettes daily and you attended a seminar on the adverse effects of smoking cigarettes. The video was so motivating and encouraging that you were determined to gradually reduce the number you smoked a day until you finally stop smoking. You came home and told your parents your decision and informed them that you would start the next day to implement your plans. In the morning, you could not put your plans into action as you met your friends for breakfast who also smoke. Six months after, you are smoking more cigarettes a day than when you first had the intention to gradually reduce to a stop.

The law of diminishing intent is another way of saying that procrastination is a thief of time and an enemy of progress. You promised yourself to earn honors at school, and you were excited at the opportunities that would come your way because of them. You were admitted into the university, but lost enthusiasm over time. You just flowed along with everyone else, doing enough studying just to get by.

As I wrote this book, I realized that I have on many occasions been slowed down by this very law. I am equally guilty. The passion in me was so strong when I started writing, but it waned a few times. Now, it is even stronger as I write the concluding chapters because I keep focusing on the young people I hope to help with what I write. I know the vast, untapped potential in each youth—each teenager who chooses to drink the weekend away rather than study or read. I want to give them the hope of a brighter, better future—there is more to life, there are dreams to rediscover, there are traits every person can take for their own, and there are hard decisions to make on the way toward a culture of positive change. I believe every person has the capacity to become a success!

How do you avoid the law of diminishing intent? It's simple. Strike while the iron is hot. Don't delay. Start writing the article in your heart. Draw up plans to start a business. Start from where you are with what you have. Don't postpone making that important phone call any longer. There is no better time to start than now. The first step is the most important. Grab every opportunity as they come. Do not put off until tomorrow what you need to do today. Utilize the power of now. Act when emotion is high. Every delay reduces the intensity of desire.

Take Charge Now

Most people work until they are sixty-five years or more in order to earn a worthwhile pension. The less fortunate ones who did not have a pensionable job or where the government is too corrupt to administer a pension, continue to work even after retirement age. The pension that accrues depends on the number of years of pensionable service, the basic salary, and the pension policy. In unstable governments, the pension may never get to the person who spent most of his or her life in service. The pension program puts a person's retirement into the hands of the government or some third party-managed pension fund. In some corrupt governments in developing countries, retirees queue up begging to be paid their due pension after over thirty-five years of service. As pathetic as this seems, a pension fund remains a good plan for retirement.

Imagine a person like Richard Branson, the owner of the Virgin Brand, would he depend on the government to hand out monthly pension money to him? The answer is no. Branson has taken care of his retirement through dividends from his numerous investments. Everyone can take charge of their retirement. There is so much opportunity in the world today that enables anybody to shape their retirement. To take charge of your retirement is to create a source of regular income that continues even after retirement from active service—this income is not a hand out from the government or a pension fund.

J.K. Rowling, author of the Harry Potter books, got the idea to write the series while she waited for four hours for a delayed train. When she finished her manuscript, twelve publishing houses rejected to publish it. Finally one accepted her book to publish with a condition that she pay about $1,200 in advance. The woman who once lived on social security is today among the richest women in Great Britain. She went to work immediately on an idea and did not allow the law of diminishing intent to destroy the idea. She took charge of her retirement. J.K. Rowling will never have to seek government hand outs because she did not let an idea elude her. She put it into action.

I know people who have stayed at jobs they hate just because they were twenty years away from pension. Nothing can be more miserable than to stick to a job you hate only to be counting the years to retirement. This unfortunately, is the case with many people.

It is possible to retire early and retire rich. No employer can pay you better than yourself. The best employer is you. The best pension is the one that guarantees financial independence. There is no financial independence from government pension or from the private sector pension fund. Financial independence only comes from an individual's strategic financial plan and action. Take charge of your retirement by starting your own business or investing savings from your employment.

Today, the Internet is making more people millionaires than any other business sector. Young people are developing apps and selling online to millions of people. Imagine an app that is sold for just $1 per download. It means that you would become a millionaire if one million people download the app. That is how easy it is to become a millionaire. It only takes one idea to create a solution to a problem. It may simply be to develop or improve an existing system, and you may have created for yourself an unending stream of income.

The best employer is you.

One of the ways to plan for retirement is to seek to improve the lives of others. No one can get rich himself unless he enriches others in the process. Businesses like McDonalds, Coca-Cola, KFC, etc. started small or as family businesses. Today these businesses have become the sources of income for many families around the world. In return, these businesses have provided wealth to the owners. Those who create jobs are more likely to have a secure retirement than those who look for jobs already created by others. Employers of labor receive dividends at retirement while employees receive pensions at retirement. The difference between the two is usually overwhelming.

Another way to take charge of your retirement now is to create sources of passive income. This income does not require your active participation. Money, in the form of royalties, from these sources would simply roll into your bank account even while you are sleeping. One way to create a passive income is to write a book. I believe everybody is qualified to write a book and everybody can write a book. This is because everybody has a story to tell. Do you love your pets? Write a book on your experience caring and loving them. Do you play golf or watch those playing golf? Write a book about your golfing experiences—it could be technical or even humorous. Have you had some bad experiences with binge drinking? Tell others of this experience and warn them not to make your mistake. Are you a comic artist? Put the ideas together into a book. Books continue to generate royalties even after the author passes.

The Internet is a global market like no other. It does not require a physical office or warehouse. It only requires Internet access. Using the Internet, you can get to potential customers from all the continents of the world in any single day. The only challenge is the product. What product could you present to customers? To create a continuous stream of passive income, Internet business must transcend beyond selling items on eBay. It requires creating a product, Website, or even a blog. The Website must have useful information that keeps visitors coming back to the site. If this is the case, you can monetize the site using platforms like Google AdSense. This system allows Google to place advertisements on the site and in return pays the site owner when visitors click on the ads. This is cool, isn't it?

Be smart and take charge of your retirement. Plan big for it. Look beyond merely receiving government hand outs. Plan to own a yacht or a holiday home at retirement. You can't do this from pension hand outs. Begin now to take charge of how you wish your retirement to be.

And Finally

Congratulations for reading up to this point. This means you have decided to live a meaningful existence. By the end of this last chapter, you will have in your possession the same tools that the great achievers of this world had.

I have come to understand that the person who eventually becomes the most successful person on earth and the homeless person who sits all day by the highway begging for money have the same equal opportunity for success or failure. It's very easy to misunderstand this point by quickly pointing at those who were born in wealthy homes as being privileged and can not to be compared to those who were born in very poor homes. Being born in a rich home is only leverage, not an advantage. Some may even classify being born in a wealthy home as a disadvantage.

When I was attending the university, a majority of the failures were those who came from very rich homes. Those of us from not very rich homes attached much more importance to our university career. We took our destiny into our hands because there was no alternative if we failed. Our colleagues from rich families could easily drop out of the university to work in a family business. It could therefore be a disadvantage rather than an advantage to come from a wealthy family.

I have heard that the reason why some youths live on the streets and are involved in gangs is because they come from broken families. This actually is an excuse rather than a reason. For such youths, I shall hastily point them to the current president of the United States of America, Barack Obama, who I mentioned previously but is worth highlighting again. He came from a broken family, being abandoned by his father and later his mother. He lost his identity and was in search of his identity until he became the U.S. president. Even as a president, he was embarrassed by some to produce his birth certificate. Obama could have used his loss of identity to become a hooligan or a street bad boy. Most people would understand had he succumbed to hard drugs and gang crime. Despite his background, he was determined to be successful, and he is now the number one citizen of the world today.

Success does not depend on race, geography, color, or background. Success is equally accessible to anyone who plays by its rules. Everybody has the same twenty-four hours in a day. The rules of success do not recognize color, race, geographical location, or educational background. Every great and successful man or woman apply these same rules. As you read these rules, allow them to penetrate into your psyche. Apply them, and you shall get the same result as others before you—success.

Rule No. 1: There must be a purpose.

To become successful, you must be driven by a purpose. An understanding that there is more to life than just mere existence leads you in search for the purpose of your life. You have a positive contribution to make in your community and in this world. You are not here on earth by chance. There is a specific design for your life. If you are a Christian, you believe that God created all life, including human beings. Most Christians are taught that God has a plan for their lives. This belief is based on a verse in the Bible (Jeremiah 1:5) where God says that before a person was formed in the mother's womb, God knew the person and had a plan for the person. This is the reason most Christians are taught to read the Bible from which they receive guidance on how to discover their purpose. I believe that God is the Creator of life and that God has a purpose, an assignment, for every person born. Before a child is conceived in the mother's womb, there is an assignment and a purpose for that child. No child is an accident. Terminating pregnancy simply because the mother does not want a child means an abortion of a specific assignment unique to that child.

Examples of assignments and purposes: The discovery of social networking through a student's experiment on the Internet revolutionized the world's communication capacity. Henry Ford's purpose was to make functional and inexpensive automobiles, which led him to develop the first assembly line technique of mass production. He revolutionized the automobile industry. Bill Gates, co-founder of Microsoft, revolutionized the personal computer industry. At a time when computers were owned solely by big organizations, Bill Gates was driven by a purpose to make computers accessible for individual purchase. Gates created the Personal Computer (PC) revolution. He retired from Microsoft and established the Bill and Melinda Gates Foundation that provides funds for eradicating diseases and providing better lives for the poor worldwide. His Microsoft Corporation made him rich and provided the money he needed to achieve his life assignment and purpose.

I understand that many people still remain confused about their purpose in life. It is very easy for someone to go after a wrong purpose and suffer frustration or lack of fulfillment. Many people are in the wrong career or job. Others are in a wrong marriage or relationship. My job, therefore, would be incomplete if I simply tell you that every successful person is driven by a purpose and not tell you how to discover your purpose. Some ideas have already been mentioned in previous chapters, others are in this final chapter.

There are many signs around you to help you discover your purpose or assignment in life. For instance, Bill Gates saw children in developing nations die of malaria, polio, and other diseases that could be eradicated. He was moved with compassion and took steps to change the access to medical care in those nations.

One way to discover your purpose is when you feel a burning desire to improve or change a bad situation. Another way to discover your purpose is to ask yourself and also try to answer this question, *What will I achieve here on earth that will make me feel fulfilled and die a happy person?* Another similar question, *What will I be remembered for after I am gone from this world?* These are very deep questions. A sincere answer to these questions will point to your purpose and assignment in life. To help direct you toward answering these two deep questions, I shall tell a story of my experience.

When I finished my first university degree, I asked myself, *What next?,* like many other young graduates ask. It became obvious to me that I would henceforth make decisions concerning my actions, and I did not want to make a wrong decision. At that time, I did not know that I was born with a purpose for my life as no one ever told me that. I did not know that I had a role to play in history and in this world. I thought I was doing pretty good, having completed my university education at an early age. My only plan was to look for a good job and work to get money.

It was at this stage in my life that my cousin gave me a book to read. The book was titled, *In Pursuit of Purpose* by Myles Munroe. I read this book voraciously and it changed my life forever. This book made me understand that just as a towel was designed to wipe water from the body, and the car was designed to move people and goods from one place to another, so also is each person designed with a specific purpose. His writings made me understand that I am not just occupying space—I have a specific assignment to achieve. The wisdom in the book made me feel important in the scheme of things in that I have a peculiar role to play. However, I needed to discover what my assignment was in this life. It made me begin to think that I was born for a reason; I went to university for a reason; I shall get a job and earn money for a reason. I had to find what this reason was.

The book explained that just as a car manufacturer produces an operations manual for the car, so also does every person have an operations manual from the Manufacturer. The operations manual for every individual, according to Munroe's book, is the Bible. It explained that within the Bible pages are the precepts that guide the operation, the life, of every individual.

So I started a journey in pursuit of my purpose. Within one year, I read through the entire Bible. I was desperate to find the purpose for my existence. By this time, it became obvious to me that simply getting a good job and making a lot of money would not give me fulfillment. There is more to my life than just being wealthy. I had to find the purpose for my life. One day as I lay on my bed relaxing and imagining what I would achieve in life that would give me fulfillment, the purpose dropped into my spirit. I knew immediately that it was the purpose for my life. I was so excited that I discovered it. This purpose has since then remained with me. When I first met the woman who would later become my wife, I told her what I believed my purpose was in life. She said she would partner with me to achieve the purpose. We continue to work together on the purpose to achieve it.

Rule No. 2: Purpose is not selfish.

Purpose in life is not about self but about others. It's not about amassing personal wealth but about improving the lives of others. If all a person has is money, what a wretched life that is. The driving force for Henry Ford was to make automobiles affordable to the poor and the middle class in the society. Today, Bill Gates is motivated to see people live in a better world with improved standards of living. Richard Branson is pursuing a project of giving ordinary people an outer space experience through his pet project, Virgin Galactic. There are men and women who have devoted their time and energy toward discovering the cure for AIDS. Purpose tends to improve the lives of others. There is a popular saying that a person who contributes to the prosperity of others must prosper in return. While a person's purpose seeks to improve the quality of others, it also improves the quality of the person.

If all you have is money, what a wretched life that is.

Purpose extends beyond acquiring money for vacations and providing for the immediate family. Providing a good life for the family is the primary responsibility of every parent, but responsibility is different from purpose in life. Purpose is unique to each individual.

Jesus Christ, who is the Son of God, said, *"The reason* [purpose] *the Son of God appeared was to destroy the devil's work."* While Jesus lived here on earth, he saw great wickedness among the people. Women were stoned to death for adultery. There was strong racial discrimination; some people saw themselves as superior to others. Jesus therefore was born to show the people how to live in love with one another. He lived his life as a model for every person to emulate. The Bible documents the life and activities of Jesus. His purpose in life was not about himself but about all others; to destroy the works of the devil in the lives of people being tormented and persecuted. Purpose is not selfish.

Rule No. 3: You need a sound mind.

A sound mind is a mental state of equilibrium. Creative ideas emerge from a sound mind. Most inventors utilize the power of a sound mind. A sound mind is your ability and capacity to make right decisions. A person under the influence of alcohol or drugs has lost the capacity to make sound decisions and ultimately the ability to create wealth.

Every person performs best with a sound mind. Your state of mind is a direct reflection of your performance in school, at work, in the family, and in relationships. I had a very close friend in my university days. He had a girlfriend who was attending another university. At that time, my friend had a problem in his relationship with the girl. The girl had told my friend that the relationship was over and my friend was very much disturbed and wanted things sorted out. I recall one occasion when I went into the café with him for a meal. We both ordered our meal with some drinks. When the meals came, we were just about to start eating when he said he could not eat, he had lost his appetite. Before I could ask more questions, he told me that he would see me later and walked out of the café. It was much later that my friend told me that he went to the girlfriend's school after he left me in the café. Unfortunately, that relationship was not mended. It was over. It affected my friend's academic performance and also caused him sleepless nights.

A Culture of Positive Change

The importance of a sound mind for a successful life cannot be overemphasized. The major reason some people can't sleep is lack of a sound mind. It is also a major reason some people lose their appetite. Without a sound mind, a student cannot retain what he or she reads. It is also the major reason for intolerance in most families. Success is not complete without a sound mind. Having a sound mind allows you to enjoy your success.

There was a time when I struggled to sleep. I discovered these bouts were a result of actions I took that part of me said that I should not have taken, or because I was seriously considering taking some actions that I did not totally agree were proper. As a result, my mind wandered off thinking about such action leading to my struggling to fall asleep. Lack of good sleep affected my next day activities. As a result, I decided to give up anything that would take sleep away from me. Since then I am delighted each time I go to bed and fall asleep immediately with no struggle.

One thing that helps me is to ensure I have peace with myself, my environment, and with people. A verse from the Bible is my guide: *"So I strive always to keep my conscience clear before God and man"* (Acts 24:16). I try my best to keep my conscience void of any offense with people and God. This guarantees my soundness and peace of mind.

Another principle for peace of mind that is greatly helpful is the following statement: *"Do not be anxious about anything, but in every situation, by prayer and petition, with thanksgiving, present your requests to God. And the peace of God, which transcends all understanding, will guard your hearts and your minds in Christ Jesus"* (Philippians 4:6-7).

I have learned not to be anxious about anything. Some of my friends and relatives often accuse me of being slow in getting things accomplished. It is a wonderful feeling when people around you are anxious and fretting—yet you are calm and relaxed over the same situation.

Rule No. 4: You must be a hard worker.

Successful people are not lazy. Most are addicted to hard work. Art Williams was a high school head coach, and his wife taught high school English. He built a newly formed team into champions in three years. As coach, if any of his team members said, "I can't," he made the player to do three push-ups as punishment. He told his team that hard work does not kill. Coach Williams was introduced to the concept of Term Life Insurance by his cousin. Williams studied the concept, which was a simpler and a cheaper alternative to Whole Life Assurance. He decided to sell Term Life Insurance on a part-time basis while he kept his coaching job. Williams later went full time selling Term Insurance, and eventually turned the concept into a business known as A.L. Williams Company. His company grew to become the largest seller of life insurance in the U.S. In ten years, his company was a billion-dollar company. As one of America's billionaires, Williams said the philosophy that can turn a concept into a fortune is wrapped up in one statement, "All you can do is all you can do."

The second part states that 'All you can do is enough'. In the statement lies the difference between winning and losing; a wealthy person and a poor person. Winners do a little more than losers. The wealthy person does a little more than the poor person. The reason people are not successful is because they did not do all they could do. A person cannot do more than the person can do. However, we have to stretch ourselves to the full extent of our reach. To be successful, all we need to do is to do all that we can do, not more and not less.

This philosophy asserts that anyone can grow wealth from a simple idea in which the person is passionate about. Williams said that he considered his business of selling Term Insurance as a crusade because he was passionately excited about it and he believed in it. The numerous 'no' answers he received from prospective clients were not strong enough to deter him. The more negative responses, the more he increased the number of people to whom he spoke.

There is an ancient principle of success that has been applied by all successful people. This principle has stood the test of time and works for whosoever applies it to their business. It simply states, *"Do you see someone skilled (or diligent) in their work? They will serve before kings; they will not serve before officials of low rank."* This timeless truth is recorded in the Bible, Proverbs 22:29. Every successful man and woman have applied this truth. Diligence is the virtue of hard work. Empires and great businesses have been built through diligence, commitment, and hard work. No matter what it is you are doing, diligence brings you to the top. In academics, diligence and hard work puts a student at top of the class; in employment, it earns an employee promotions; in business, growth; in politics, it makes the leader. If you wish to stand with kings, apply hard work and diligence to whatever good work you are doing.

Rule No. 5: Don't allow the fear of failure to stop you from trying.

Failure is not trying and failing, but failing to try. The difference between a successful person and an unsuccessful person is this: for a person to become successful, the joy of success is greater than the fear of failure, so the person keeps trying until he or she succeeds. For a person to become unsuccessful, the fear of failure is greater than the joy of success, so the person fails to try.

Remember, Thomas Edison performed his incandescent light experiment about 10,000 times before he eventually succeeded. He was motivated by the joy of success and not deterred by the fear of failing. For this reason, he is well-known as a successful man in history, having over 2,000 patents worldwide with over 1,000 of those patents in the United States. According to Thomas Edison, each failed experiment taught him how it would *not* work and took him one step closer to how it *would* work.

People like Richard Branson would tell you that success requires a person to be "thick-skinned" and not be afraid of trying new ideas. Success often requires thinking outside the box and to having the guts to try the idea. As long as you start all over to try an idea each time it does not work out, it is not regarded as failure. It only becomes a failed idea when you give up trying. No doubt you have heard the statement, "If at first you don't succeed, try, try again." This saying is the secret of most successful people.

Never give up on an idea. Many destinies have been lost due to people being too afraid to try the creative ideas in their heads. Sometimes the friends we keep kill our ideas even before we are able to try them. When the idea of flying a heavy metal object in the air was conceived, many scientists said it was impossible due to the pull of gravity. The Wright brothers defied all odds and developed a human-controlled flying machine—the airplane. The accomplishment did not come easy as they had many failed trials before they finally achieved success.

Rule No. 6: Education is not a prerequisite for success.

Through education, accumulated knowledge, skills, and values are deliberately passed on to another individual. Education is a process that is designed to have a formative effect on individuals from a tender age. A child is taught from a tender age societal values that are preserved and passed from generation to generation, such as be polite and do not steal. We are taught in school about scientific matters such as the gravitational force and that the earth is spherical. Depending on a person's choice of career, there are educational curriculums designed to impact knowledge toward achieving a specific goal. A person is said to be formally educated after successfully completing the curriculum and passing the final examination.

The world is full of people who are formally educated only to end up in some form of routine job. Although the world needs all types of formally educated people in all types of jobs, the world also needs people who have the courage to stretch the boundaries of formal education and think outside the box. These are the dreamers and the inventors. To think outside the box is to tap from the potential that lies within the mind of every individual. It means being creative and original. The world does not celebrate those who are formally educated. It only celebrates those who dare to be different by thinking outside the box.

I have come to observe that some of the greatest men and women in the world were and are people who put aside formal education. Most of them were not formally educated. They refused to conform and rather reached into the deep resource of their minds to produce creative ideas that are celebrated worldwide.

The world cannot forget Thomas Edison in a hurry. He is one of the greatest inventors the world ever produced. One of his legacies is the incandescent light. Thomas suffered from partial deafness and lacked formal education. He believed that he had something to live for and reached into the deep resources of his mind by thinking outside the box.

J.D. Rockefeller is believed to be the richest man in history. He had hoped to go to college but had to drop out of high school in order to work and to support his family. By the age of twenty-five years, he already had a refinery. Without formal education, J D Rockefeller assessed the great wealth of his mind to establish his great empire and to employ the educated folks.

The story of Bill Gates, the co-founder of Microsoft Corporation is known to most people all over the world because of the revolution of the personal computer. Bill had special interest in programming and would like to try new things. Although he had admission in Harvard College, he had to drop out because of his attachment to programming machine. Today, Microsoft is a house-hold name because someone refused to conform.

Similar story goes for Steve Jobs who was the co-founder of Apple Inc. After graduating from high school, Steve Jobs enrolled in Reed College, Portland, Oregon but had to drop out after just one semester. The success story of his inventions that include iPod, iPhone, iPad is the testimony of a man who dared to be different.

I have just mentioned some of the world greatest inventors and business people. The list is unending. Most of these men and women did not have formal education. They escaped the mental captivity imposed through formal education. This enabled them to reach down into the deep resource of the mind. Exploring this resource positively transforms a person into a creator. Humans are by nature creative beings but this ability is sometimes hindered by the formative effect of education. Education teaches conformity. Conformity with the world is never celebrated.

The world only celebrates those who are different. If you really wish to excel in life, be prepared to stretch the boundaries.

Conclusion

I hope you have been inspired by the people mentioned in the book and by the fact that you can bring about a culture of positive change in your life, the life of your family, your community, region, country, and the world. You have all that you need to do so already within you—your potential lies waiting to be accessed and put to work.

Rediscover your childhood dreams and become a world-changer. The luxury of time is not on your side—you must act immediately to set plans in motion. You must today choose to make the hard decisions and adopt the traits of successful people, thrusting you into a unique and God-given destiny that no one but you can fulfill.

* * *

The following are success nuggets that I think you will find helpful as you start your journey toward achieving your goals and successful living. Seriously consider each one, and then write a few thoughts about how you can incorporate that nugget into your current lifestyle or your future aspirations.

You have got a good life ahead of you. Best wishes for an exciting journey—I hope you enjoy every moment of it!

Appendix A

Success Nuggets

SUCCESS NUGGET #1
Work on yourself more than you work on your job.

SUCCESS NUGGET #2
Give a little more than you are paid for.

SUCCESS NUGGET #3
Spend an hour every day studying something new about your current job.

SUCCESS NUGGET #4
Make yourself a friendly person.

SUCCESS NUGGET #5
You have to be mentally prepared to receive success.

___

SUCCESS NUGGET #6
To test your preparedness for success, what would you do if you inherited $1 million?

___

SUCCESS NUGGET #7
Success does not lie in the amount of money you possess but in what you do with the money.

___

SUCCESS NUGGET #8
It is better to have ideas and wait for money to execute the ideas, than to have money and no idea about how to use it.

___

SUCCESS NUGGET #9
Success is first created in the mind before it is created in the physical. If you can't see it on the inside, you won't see it on the outside.

___

SUCCESS NUGGET #10
Opportunity comes equally to every person but only those prepared for it see it. And only those who act on it, get it.

SUCCESS NUGGET #11
Searchers are finders. Only those who search, find.

SUCCESS NUGGET #12
Every person's success growth is directly proportional to the person's knowledge.

Points to Ponder

- *List ten areas of improvement in your life, career or job within the last 6 months.*
- *What is something you can do tomorrow that will improve your job performance and get the attention of your boss and colleagues?*
- *How prepared are you mentally and emotionally to receive success?*
- *List 10 things you would achieve or do if you were given $1 million today.*
- *Write down a clear description of the success you see in your mind and that you want to achieve.*
- *Do you see opportunity where others do not? Are you ready to open the door the next time opportunity knocks?*

SUCCESS NUGGET #13
A person who is emotionally stable achieves more success.

SUCCESS NUGGET #14
A sound mind is instrumental in achieving success.

SUCCESS NUGGET #15
Success is a process, not an event.

SUCCESS NUGGET #16
Real success must have a successor.

SUCCESS NUGGET #17
Success is no respecter of persons.

SUCCESS NUGGET #18
The road to success is often less bumpy if you follow someone with proven success.

SUCCESS NUGGET #19
It helps to have a mentor on entry into Success Lane and to have a successor on exit from Success Lane.

SUCCESS NUGGET #20
If you change for the better, everything will change for you.

Points to Ponder

- *Do you have a mentor with proven success record to follow after his years of experience?*
- *How many books of success by proven authors do you plan to read in the next six months?*
- *What changes are you willing to make to improve your life and personality?*

SUCCESS NUGGET #21
Don't be afraid to ask. Only those who ask receive.

_____

SUCCESS NUGGET #22
Don't be afraid to knock. Only those who knock have doors opened for them.

_____

SUCCESS NUGGET #23
Always explore all opportunities that exist in your current job before seeking greener pastures.

_____

SUCCESS NUGGET #24
Physical and material prosperity is inexplicably tied to the limit set in your mind—it can't grow beyond it.

_____

SUCCESS NUGGET #25
Prosperity only stays with good manager. It quickly vanishes from those who manage it badly.

_____

SUCCESS NUGGET #26
Success will seldom remain with anyone who doesn't understand the value of success.

Points to Ponder

- *Do you have the courage to knock and to ask? What would you ask and who would you ask?*
- *In your current job, what opportunities do you see for your growth?*
- *Are you a good manager of the prosperity you currently enjoy?*

SUCCESS NUGGET #27
Diamonds don't look like diamonds in their raw state—they are dirty and impure.

SUCCESS NUGGET #28
There are no bad jobs; but our attitudes make them good or bad.

SUCCESS NUGGET #29
You can be good at anything if you put over 10,000 hours of work into it.

SUCCESS NUGGET #30
Don't rest on your laurels once they are won.

SUCCESS NUGGET #31
If you wait for perfect conditions, you will never get anything accomplished.

A Culture of Positive Change

Points to Ponder

- *Are you willing to get your hands dirty doing your job?*
- *Are you ready to put in additional hours of learning to get better at your job?*
- *How willing are you to step up to the next level at work, at home, at your hobby?*

_____
_____

SUCCESS NUGGET #32
Action makes dreams become reality.

SUCCESS NUGGET #33
All you can do is all you need to be successful. Just do all you can do.

SUCCESS NUGGET #34
If you do all you can do every day in a meaningful activity, you will become successful in that endeavor.

SUCCESS NUGGET #35
Hard work does not mean working until you sweat—it means putting a little extra effort in after others stop.

SUCCESS NUGGET #36
Hard work does not kill, it give you leverage.

SUCCESS NUGGET #37
To every person there are 24 hours: 8 hours for sleep, 8 hours for work, and what you do with the remaining 8 hours determines your status in life.

SUCCESS NUGGET #38
Every person is in a personal race against time.

SUCCESS NUGGET #39
What you do every day is the value you exchange for a day of your life.

SUCCESS NUGGET #40
Every day that passes by is one day removed from your life.

SUCCESS NUGGET #41
When you look back over your life, what you see is the value you have exchanged for the years you have lived.

SUCCESS NUGGET #42
Unfortunately, time does not wait for us while we sleep or go on vacation. It keep moving and never takes a break.

SUCCESS NUGGET #43
We can invest our time, spend it, or waste it. Time invested brings the best returns.

SUCCESS NUGGET #44
When you look back over your life, what you see is the proof of the time you invested. Time merely spent or wasted has little or nothing to show for it.

Points to Ponder

- *Are you doing all you can do today?*
- *Are you putting a little extra effort above that of your colleagues and competitors?*
- *How do you use the 8 hours in a day? Do you invest it or waste it?*
- *Are you wasting your days or are you using every day to its fullest to achieve your dreams?*
- *What value did you add to your life today? List 5 achievements you have accomplished in the last 5 years.*
- *What are you investing your time in? Is this the best use of your time?*

SUCCESS NUGGET #45
A person's primary limitation is his mentality.

SUCCESS NUGGET #46
You may never understand your potential until a small wall separates you from life and death. You will be amazed how easy you will climb over the wall.

SUCCESS NUGGET #47
Your thinking determines your outcome.

SUCCESS NUGGET #48
The words you speak create the atmosphere around you—be it negative or positive.

SUCCESS NUGGET #49
Your mind listens to every word that you speak and acts on it.

SUCCESS NUGGET #50
It is difficult to succeed beyond the level of your mind's aspiration.

John Iroh

SUCCESS NUGGET #51
As crazy as it may seem—think BIG.

Points to Ponder

- *Have you been limited because you think you can't? Change your thinking to "I can."*
- *Do you sometimes say negative words such as "I can't do it"? Rather say, "How can I do it."*
- *How BIG are you thinking?*

A Culture of Positive Change

SUCCESS NUGGET #52
Dreamers are pacesetters. They shape the world. If you want to go beyond the limit—be a dreamer.

SUCCESS NUGGET #53
To be successful, you must avoid the companion of failures.

SUCCESS NUGGET #54
Do not reveal your dream to a dream killer.

SUCCESS NUGGET #55
Do not misunderstand yourself when others misunderstand you.

Points to Ponder

- *What kind of friends do you keep around you? Motivators or dream killers?*
- *Do you put too much faith and trust in those around you rather than yourself?*

SUCCESS NUGGET #56
To be successful, you must do the right thing and not necessarily the good thing.

SUCCESS NUGGET #57
The wealthiest place that exists on earth is the mind of a human being.

SUCCESS NUGGET #58
From the deep resource of the mind has been created all that exists on the face of the earth today.

SUCCESS NUGGET #59
The deep resource of the mind is best accessed in the atmosphere of tranquillity. If you do, you will be amazed at the success potential that exists within you.

SUCCESS NUGGET #60
The mind is like a deep ocean. The deeper you go, the more you see. The only difference is that you will never get to the end of its depth.

SUCCESS NUGGET #61
You will never run out of resources to build an empire in your mind.

_____
_____

SUCCESS NUGGET #62
If you translate the pictures of your mind to paper, it becomes easier to translate it from paper to reality.

_____
_____

SUCCESS NUGGET #63
The mind always processes the information you feed into it. To be successful, you must feed your mind with information on success.

_____
_____

SUCCESS NUGGET #64
The mind can be programmed for success. Just feed it on success.

_____
_____

Points to Ponder

- *Do you set a time of tranquility to access the deep resource of your mind?*
- *Do you feed your mind with junk or with success?*

- *Do you have an image of your aspirations in its finished form developed in your mind? Can you translate it onto paper?*

A Culture of Positive Change

SUCCESS NUGGET #65
Saving is the attitude of the rich.

_____
_____

SUCCESS NUGGET #66
A person who cannot save a portion of his earnings cannot accumulate wealth.

_____
_____

SUCCESS NUGGET #67
Wisdom desires that you sow your seed and not eat it.

_____
_____

SUCCESS NUGGET #68
You will get richer if you refuse to allow your expenses to grow as your earnings grow.

_____
_____

SUCCESS NUGGET #69
Just like time, we can invest our money, spend it, or waste it. Money invested brings the best returns.

_____
_____

Points to Ponder

- *Do your expenses increase each time your income increases?*
- *Is saving a portion of your income something you do diligently or sporadically?*
- *Are you investing, spending, or wasting your time and money?*

_____
_____

A Culture of Positive Change

SUCCESS NUGGET #70
A person's wealth does not lie in the fat wallet but in the income that keeps refilling the wallet once spent.

SUCCESS NUGGET #71
A person's wealth does not depend on the saving in the bank account, but on the things the person wisely invests the savings into.

SUCCESS NUGGET #72
To be rich and wealthy, you must consider how every penny of your savings would replicate itself through wise investment.

SUCCESS NUGGET #73
Financial independence begins when you have enough regular income from your invested savings that you do not need to work anymore.

SUCCESS NUGGET #74
A person's wealth is not in the bank vault but in the gold stream of income that continuously flows into the person's savings account.

SUCCESS NUGGET #75
Every earning in itself has the capability to multiply if put into profitable investments. Savings kept in a bank vault increase only by the interest it earns—but there is more capability.

SUCCESS NUGGET #76
The foremost principle of investment is the security for the principal.

Points to Ponder

- *In what profitable investment can you put your savings? Is there a better investment than the bank's interest on savings?*
- *Does your investment guarantee security of your principal?*

SUCCESS NUGGET #77
Every accomplishment is preceded by desire. The desire must be strong, simple, and definite.

SUCCESS NUGGET #78
A person who desires to have a profit of $1,000 from his business is most likely to succeed faster than a person who desires to have a successful business.

SUCCESS NUGGET #79
The person who seeks to learn more of his or her craft shall be richly rewarded. This principle is proved over and over again.

SUCCESS NUGGET #80
Wealth brings to its possessor responsibility and respect from others.

SUCCESS NUGGET #81
The price for greatness is responsibility. Greatness brings with it an equal measure of responsibility.

SUCCESS NUGGET #82
To whom much is given, much is also expected.

SUCCESS NUGGET #83
When all is said and done, the wealth you are left with is what you have given away to charity.

SUCCESS NUGGET #84
Giving to others makes us appreciate what we have, not what we have acquired.

Points to Ponder

- *Is your desire strong, simple, and definite in reaching your goals?*
- *Are you ready to accept the responsibility that comes with wealth?*
- *Are you naturally a giver, or do you need to be reminded to give to others less fortunate?*

SUCCESS NUGGET #85
A person who will become wealthy always has one thing more than someone else—a dream.

SUCCESS NUGGET #86
A person who accumulates tangible wealth must first acquire intangible wealth in the form of personal development.

SUCCESS NUGGET #87
Every person is a success waiting to happen. All the success a person shall become is stored in the person until it manifests physically. A person has to work it out.

SUCCESS NUGGET #88
Success is not the result of making money, rather making money is the result of success.

SUCCESS NUGGET #89
Success comes in direct proportion to service provided.

SUCCESS NUGGET #90
A person who contributes to the prosperity of others must prosper in return.

SUCCESS NUGGET #91
No one can get rich himself unless he enriches others.

Point to Ponder

- *Have you benefited from helping others? How?*

SUCCESS NUGGET #92
Success is built from the ground to the top. Only grave diggers start from the top and go down.

SUCCESS NUGGET #93
Gold, in its pure state is often covered with dirt and mud. A person who must acquire gold must be willing to get dirty in the process.

SUCCESS NUGGET #94
True success is measured by the service provided and not by the service received.

SUCCESS NUGGET #95
Wealth acquired can provide comfort, but fulfillment comes from the lives it has changed.

SUCCESS NUGGET #96
He is so poor that all he has is money—having only money with no good works amounts to poverty.

SUCCESS NUGGET #97
The value of money does not depend on the quantity but on what the money accomplishes.

___

SUCCESS NUGGET #98
A person may have $1 million in the bank and yet be poorer than someone who has just $1,000 in savings.

___

Points to Ponder

- *Into what service would you put your money if you have it in abundance?*
- *To start small toward achieving your aspirations, what would be the first steps you would take?*

SUCCESS NUGGET #99
Money is an obedient servant; it can be used to improve or destroy life. It can even sit and wait on you if you have no plans for it.

SUCCESS NUGGET #100
People earn money based on the value they bring into the marketplace—not for the time spent in bringing value.

SUCCESS NUGGET #101
Those who seek, find. In other words, you can't find what you don't seek.

SUCCESS NUGGET #102
Those who ask, receive. In other words, you may not receive because you don't ask.

Points to Ponder

- *How good are you at seeking and asking?*

- *Are you willing to improve the value you bring into the marketplace or to your employer and increase your earning capacity?*

_____
_____

A Culture of Positive Change

SUCCESS NUGGET #103
Each time you fail, you are one step closer to success. Celebrate each failure.

SUCCESS NUGGET #104
Never allow the fear of failure to overshadow the joy of success.

SUCCESS NUGGET #105
Trying and failing is in the domain of success, but not trying is in the domain of failure.

SUCCESS NUGGET #106
It is more honorable to try and fail than not failing through not trying.

SUCCESS NUGGET #107
Trying and failing increases a person's knowledge.

SUCCESS NUGGET #108
There is nothing as powerful as an idea whose time has come.

SUCCESS NUGGET #109
If life was a game, it is better that you played and lost than not playing at all.

SUCCESS NUGGET #110
Take rest or sleep as a necessity, not as an objective.

Points to Ponder

- *Have you learned from your mistakes and failures?*
- *How do you react when you don't get it right after many trials? Frustrated or motivated?*

A Culture of Positive Change

SUCCESS NUGGET #111
The only thing to feel good about yourself is to stretch yourself to the full capacity of your reach.

___

SUCCESS NUGGET #112
Trees grow to as high as they could possibly grow. Humans develop less than their maximum potential because of the power of choice.

___

SUCCESS NUGGET #113
Whether you make $1,000 a year or $1 million a year, as long as you did all you could possible do—that is called success.

___

SUCCESS NUGGET #114
The average person wants to get *off* the task, but the achiever wants to get *on* with the task.

___

SUCCESS NUGGET #115
As the depth of a foundation determines the height of a structure, so also the depth of a person's knowledge determines the height of a person's development.

Points to Ponder

- *Do you consider yourself as stretching yourself to full capacity of your reach?*
- *How willing are you to gain more knowledge and invest in your personal development?*

_____

_____

A Culture of Positive Change

SUCCESS NUGGET #116
You learn more by losing than you learn by winning.

SUCCESS NUGGET #117
Everything you need is within reach. Only those who reach out, grasp what they need.

SUCCESS NUGGET #118
Ideas are life-changing—whether right ideas or wrong ideas.

SUCCESS NUGGET #119
Ten years from now, you must surely arrive. But do you have a destination set?

SUCCESS NUGGET #120
Now is the time to fix the next ten years. A few daily disciplines make a world of difference.

Points to Ponder

- *Have you learned anything from losing?*

- *Have you set the destination you wish to arrive in the next ten years?*
- *How do you see yourself in ten years? What do you want to accomplish by then?*

_____

_____

A Culture of Positive Change

SUCCESS NUGGET #121
In life, we either suffer the pain of regret or the pain of discipline.

SUCCESS NUGGET #122
Whatever your hands find to do, do it with all your might.

SUCCESS NUGGET #123
If you are capable of making $500,000 and you make only $100,000—you are called a loser.

SUCCESS NUGGET #124
If you do your best and make $10,000, that is enough. Enough is doing your best.

Points to Ponder

- *Have you chosen the pain of discipline rather than the pain of regret?*
- *Are you doing enough? Are you doing all that you can do?*

SUCCESS NUGGET #125
If you believe in what you are doing, you won't quit no matter the number of failed attempts and criticisms.

SUCCESS NUGGET #126
Be careful who you meet for advice. Advice from a person of proven experience is good, while advice from a fool is doom.

SUCCESS NUGGET #127
Every failed attempt is one step closer to success; it defines the path of success.

SUCCESS NUGGET #128
The value of success is learned by the many failures prior to success.

SUCCESS NUGGET #129
Failures bring you one step closer as you walk the path of success.

A Culture of Positive Change

SUCCESS NUGGET #130
What you become is more important than what you get.

_____
_____

SUCCESS NUGGET #131
A little capital mixed with ingenuity and desire to succeed equates to success.

_____
_____

Points to Ponder

- *Who are your advisors? Are they bringing you down or lifting you up?*
- *How persistence are you at achieving your set goals? Are you deterred by failed attempts?*

_____
_____

SUCCESS NUGGET #132
Without dreams and visions, people perish.

SUCCESS NUGGET #133
Success is not in short supply. There is enough for as many as seek it.

SUCCESS NUGGET #134
Preparation precedes performance.

SUCCESS NUGGET #135
Our actions cannot be wiser than our thoughts.

SUCCESS NUGGET #136
Our thinking cannot be wiser than our understanding.

SUCCESS NUGGET #137
To achieve what you desire, time and study is required.

A Culture of Positive Change

Points to Ponder

- *How are you preparing to achieve the success you desire?*
- *Are you prepared to invest in time and study toward achieving success?*

_____

_____

SUCCESS NUGGET #138
Wealth, like a tree, grows from a tiny seed. It needs nourishment and watering to grow.

SUCCESS NUGGET #139
Our "necessary expense" will always grow to equal our income unless we protest to the contrary.

SUCCESS NUGGET #140
Wealth and riches remain with those who are selective on the desires they must gratify.

Point to Ponder

- *Do you have control over your desires, or do they control you?*

SUCCESS NUGGET #141
The person who seeks to know more of his or her craft shall be richly rewarded.

SUCCESS NUGGET #141
One hour spent each day to learn something new about your job or field of career will make you a master in that field in five years' time.

SUCCESS NUGGET #142
As the world continues to advance and progress, achievers continue to be in the front rank of progress. Those who stand still are left behind.

SUCCESS NUGGET #144
Follow the path of those with proven records of success. Under such mentorship, you acquire the wisdom of their years of experience in one month.

Points to Ponder

- *Are you moving forward as the world progresses or has life passed you by?*

- *Are you willing to invest one hour a day learning something new in the field of your endeavor?*
- *Do you have a mentor under whom you acquire wisdom of the ages?*

_____
_____

A Culture of Positive Change

SUCCESS NUGGET #145
Never allow failed attempts to cause you to lose your enthusiasm—it is the driving force to success.

SUCCESS NUGGET #146
All it takes to gain mastery is hard work and a few daily disciplines.

SUCCESS NUGGET #147
Seasons, time, chance, and policies happen to us all. It's not what happens but what we do about what happens that matters.

SUCCESS NUGGET #148
Achievers enter their day before the day comes.

SUCCESS NUGGET #149
Do you want to retire for a government pension or do you want to receive dividends from your own company?

SUCCESS NUGGET #150
Achievers decide when they retire; they also decide their own retirement package.

Points to Ponder

- *Enthusiasm and hard work—are they part of your daily lifestyle?*
- *Do you have your day planned before the day comes?*
- *What plans have you set for your retirement?*

About the Book

Many people are trapped in jobs they hate to do only to wait agonizingly for the retirement year as it crawls endlessly one year at a time. It seems like too much of misery and yet, the best such people could do is to endure the misery and wait for the due retirement. Most of our youths do not have plans beyond the next weekend.

It is possible to design your own retirement and also decide when. Youths can become achievers even before they become adults. It is possible to contribute into the society rather than depend on the society. Everyone can truly have and enjoy a successful and fulfilling life. It is never late to embrace a culture of positive change.

A Culture of Positive Change explores your potential—a resource that every person has, to achieve success. It provides guidance to help you discover your unique purpose for living. The wisdom and advice presented on every page challenge you to activate the rich deposit of ability within you and also provides ideas and suggestions about how you can become an achiever—even a celebrity.

Chapters focus on the following as well as many other topics leading to success:

- It All Begins with a Dream
- You Already Possess All You Need to Succeed
- Common Traits of Successful People
- You Have to Make the Hard Decisions
- Hints on Discovering Who You Are
- 150 "Success Nuggets"

A Culture of Positive Change contains all of the key components required to become a truly prosperous, fulfilled person. You were created to be successful!

About the Author

John Iroh is a structural engineer by professional training and resident in Aberdeen, Scotland, United Kingdom. He volunteers with organizations helping people in need of emotional support. Through personal experience and research, he is discovering the attributes required for a successful and fulfilling life. He is passionate that every person can indeed live and enjoy a successful, happy, and fulfilling life.

He conducts Empowering Sessions with youths, assisting them to become achievers. He contributes to Ezine articles as an author and expert writer.

The author may be contacted through email to irohjohn@yahoo.com or irohjohn@gmail.com

www.ingramcontent.com/pod-product-compliance
Lightning Source LLC
Chambersburg PA
CBHW052029070526
44584CB00016B/1962